Teaching Emotional Intelligence

to Children

Fifty Fun Activities For

Families, Teachers and Therapists

Lynne Namka, Ed. D.

Illustrated by Nancy Sarama

Talk, Trust & Feel Therapeutics   Tucson, Arizona

Also by Lynne Namka

The Doormat Syndrome

The Mad Family Gets Their Mads Out

How to Let Go of Your Mad Baggage

Avoiding Relapse: Catching Your Inner Con

A Gathering of Grandmothers: Words of Wisdom from Women of Spirit and Power,

Good Bye Ouchies and Grouchies, Hello Happy Feelings: EFT for Kids of All Ages

For information go to www.AngriesOut.com

Published by
Talk, Trust & Feel Therapeutics,
5398 Golder Ranch Road
Tucson, Arizona 85739

ISBN 0-9642167-3-6

Library of Congress Control Number: 2003096746

Printed in the United States of America

Teaching Children to Name, Express and Release Unhappy Feelings

Children enjoy learning through using their feelings. These lesson plans give activities to aid in learning the necessary skills of Emotional Intelligence. Ten to fifteen minutes a day teaching these activities will give your children the skills for a happier life. These lesson plans tie three areas of psychology together: Cognitive Behavioral, Jungian Psychology and the newer Energy Psychology.

The Cognitive Behavioral Approach: Cues for Teachers and Helper Words for Children

Cues from adults are a primary means of instruction for teaching social skills. Positive cues give the child who misbehaves an immediate alternative regarding what he can do differently. Adding repetitious cues to your teaching will help children learn to talk about what is bothering them. These key phrases do not belittle or shame him and help him save face by instructing him what he can do to take care of himself. They remind him to make a responsible choice to feel good about himself. They work! The constant repetition of these cues helps the child internalize the messages as his own.

Add cues to your teaching repertoire gradually by practicing one cue for several days until you hear yourself saying it automatically in response to specific children's behavior. Post several visual reminders around your room for yourself to assist your student's learning. Share these cues with the parents of the children so that they can use them at home also.

Helper Words comes from Cognitive Behavioral Psychology where negative thoughts are interrupted and replaced with healthy ways of thinking. Teaching children to do self-talk gives them positive messages to carry around with themselves. The small amount of time that you spend in rehearsing the children in the self-talk statements will save you from time spent on reprimands.

Kids need to hear these key phrases over and over again in order to learn to express their feelings. Repetition is the best way to learn a new skill. Group rehearsals via chanting, as the standard group practice done in Chinese schools, is very effective in memorization of these positive messages. The lesson plans give different Helper Words that you can teach the children through saying them out loud in unison.

Your task, if you choose to accept it, is to repeat the Helper Word phrases (choose the ones you like best) until you hear the children using them on their own. Take the time to learn and teach these statements to save you time and your voice in the long run. Helper Words and Cues are valuable motivational tools. You will find yourself becoming a more positive teacher by encouraging children to take responsibility for their own behavior.

The Energy Psychology Approach: Do It Yourself Acupressure

Johnny Carson once asked a feisty, 104 year old woman what the secret was to her longevity. She replied, "I didn't smoke or drink; I went to church and raised my family. And when something hurt, I just poked it!"

Want a quick way to help kids release stress, fears, anxiety, anger and guilt? Sometimes our body just wants poking. The Emotional Freedom Technique (EFT) is the fastest, easiest method of releasing any stress or upset. EFT is one of the new Energy Psychology techniques. EFT is easy to do. Just own the problem, say an affirmation, and tap a few acupressure points while thinking about the bad feelings or the problem. The technique demonstrates the power of the mind while using acupressure to release the negative emotions and beliefs that cause disturbances in the body's energy system.

EFT has its roots in Applied Kinesiology, Cognitive Behavioral Psychology and acupuncture. In Chinese Medicine, energy is believed to flow along meridians on the body through points that Chinese practitioners have identified. Poking or tapping certain parts of the body, while thinking and feeling upset about something, changes the energy in the meridians. Most people are amazed at how fast these techniques work to release energetic emotional blocks. The procedures are easy to learn so that you can apply them to yourself and teach them to children. See *Goodbye Ouchies and Grouchies, Hello Happy Feelings: EFT for Kids of All Ages* for the complete method. (School discounts for this book for parents are available for orders of 25 or more at www.AngriesOut.com)

Jungian Psychology: Integrating the Parts of the Personality

Play is the language of children. As they play, they learn to incorporate the necessary attitudes, values and behaviors of their culture. The activities given in these lesson plans are playful and light to show that emotions are normal.

Carl Jung believed that the human psyche is split into the *persona*, which is the aspect of the self of which we approve and with which we identify, and the *dark shadow*, that consists of those characteristics that we find hateful and unbearable. There are the normal multiple aspects of our self, which come forth in different moods and environments. Jung described the shadow as those parts of the self that are cut off from the rest but are attached just as a real shadow is attached to the body. Presenting the topics of anger and getting in trouble in a light way helps children identify with and understand their unacceptable urges and behavior. These lesson plans help children learn about their shadow parts and provide the motivation to recognize and change them.

Together these three approaches help bring negative beliefs and feelings to the surface, help children integrate and transform their unhappy and negative experiences in their lives, and when they are used along with play therapy, they give a well-rounded program

Confidentiality and Other Legalities

Providing a safe setting for children to share feelings can bring up an occasional story from a child where others could possibly be punished in a court of law. Review your state's laws on reporting child abuse laws so that you are up to date on the legalities of protecting children from criminal acts. Remember that all actions of others are alleged until they are proven by a court of law, or until the abuser admits the abusive behavior.

Discuss confidentiality with the children and tell them that what anyone says in group is to stay here and are not to be shared. Remind the children that what they talk about should be considered private and not discussed with anyone later.

If you suspect that the child might have been abused from the story he tells, just ask for the feeling and do not encourage him to go into the details. You do not need to know the "what, where and why" of serious events of suspected abuse that the child experienced. The intent of these lesson plans is for release of feelings in a safe environment with an empathetic adult who can teach them some coping skills.

The two types of children's stories that need not be discussed in with other children present include two categories:

- Events which are not illegal but do not need to be aired in a group: If a child brings up an issue that is best discussed in private, just say "Super Hero Bear just told me that he wanted to talk with you about this later (or wanted you to talk about this with the guidance counselor.")

- Events which might involve illegal acts: Asking the child questions about a criminal act that happened to him could "contaminate" the information should there need to be an investigation by a children's services agency. If you get a bad feeling in the pit of your stomach as the child describes an incident, go to the feeling level quickly (Ask how did you feel?) and move on quickly with the teaching. Discuss what the child said with another professional to determine if authorities need to be contacted.

I AM MANY PARTS

Happy Part

The Part That Knows It is Loved

Baby Part

Sad Part

Super Hero Part

Mad Part

Trouble Part

Bad Feeling Part

Stuffed Animals to Enhance the Lesson Plans

Kids love stuffed animals and identify with them easily. Presenting the emotions and parts of the personality gives children metaphors that they understand. Find stuffed animals that represent the different parts of the personality. Any stuffed animal or puppet will work (puppets take longer to put on and take off the hands so I recommend using stuffed animals.)

Don't sweat over finding the "exact" animal to fit the part. Once you introduce the different parts, the children believe in the part and quickly catch on to the concepts. Sometimes I just put a lot of different animals on the table and ask the children to choose the ones they think fit the emotion. You might ask the children to bring extra stuffed animals from home that will fit the different emotions. Some families might be willing to donate stuffed animals.

Find stuffed animals that represent these different parts of the personality:

Sad Part: Draw tears on a dog with a magic marker

Mad Part: Crab or any stuffed animal that looks angry

Trouble Part: A spider or any stuffed animal that has a "rascal" look.

Bad Feelings Part: Any stuffed animal that you stitch the mouth downward and the head on the chest to indicate shame.

Happy Part: Clown or happy face

Baby Part: Small, sweet looking stuffed animal

Super Hero Bear: Any bear that you add a cape to. Capes can be made from any material. Cut with pinking shears to avoid having to sew.

Instructions for the Parents of the Children You Teach

Prepare the parents so they can support the changes the children will be making. Send the following Dar Parents letter, the article on Emotional Intelligence and description and pictures of The Emotional Freedom Technique to the parents so they will know about the lessons their children will be learning. You may copy any parts of this curriculum to share with the parents of the children you work with!

You may want to keep the children's finished drawing pages and worksheets and put them in a folder for the children to keep. Spread the word about Helper Words to boost self-esteem and performance! Start a Super Hero Bear Fan Club at home.

Dear parents,

We are starting an exciting new project here in our classroom to teach children Emotional Intelligence. According to Mayer and Salovey, "Emotional intelligence is the ability to perceive emotions, to access and generate emotions so as to assist thought, to understand emotions and emotional knowledge, and to reflectively regulate emotions so as to promote emotional and intellectual growth." People who are clued into their Emotional Intelligence interpret and use their feelings to think and act appropriately according to the needs of the social situation. Emotional Intelligence is said to be more important than IQ in becoming successful in today's world.

The children will participate in activities that help them learn to use their emotions in positive ways. Here are some of the skills necessary for Emotional Intelligence and thereby obtaining success in life:

- Emotional Self-Awareness and Self-Management—Regulating anxiety, stress and anger and inhibit impulsivity. Learning self-soothing and stress management techniques to handle inner distress.

- Social Awareness—Recognizing verbal and nonverbal cues of the negative emotions of others. Having empathy and understanding and being tolerant of others and their feelings. Refraining from actions that hurt others.

- Self-discipline— Being conscientious and demonstrating hard work controlling negative emotions, words, actions and impulses.

- Persistence and Motivation—Being willing to act on meaningful priorities and giving good effort. Continuing to persevere on hard work with determination even when confronted with failure.

- Trust Worthiness and Honesty— Having integrity, telling the truth and admitting wrongdoing. Being truthful with yourself and owning your mistakes and feelings is the basic foundation for honesty.

The Psychological Research on Happiness

After years of studying people with problems, psychologists are now studying happy people who are making a success of their lives. The research shows that these skills are necessary to create happiness in life:

- Being competent at what you do
- Stopping errors in thinking
- Dealing with feelings of inner distress
- Negotiating conflict
- Being connected to friends
- Having faith in something greater than yourself
- Taking responsibility and owning and changing mistakes
- Using self-regulatory skills to continue when work becomes hard

Our curriculum has fun activities that incorporate many of these skills. The activities are based on giving your children a good foundation for dealing with their feelings. The three approaches that I will use to give your children skills for good self-esteem are drawn from Cognitive Behavioral Psychology, Jungian Psychology and The Emotional Freedom Technique.

Helper Words and Sharing Feelings—The Cognitive Behavioral Approach

Children who share feelings in safe and appropriate ways feel good about themselves. Sharing feelings gives children a sense of control over the things that go wrong in their lives. Super Hero Bear will be visiting our class to help your child understand him or herself better. Super Hero Bear teaches the children the "I feel ____, when you ____." formula for getting feelings out. (I feel (angry, upset, etc.) when you (hit me, raise your voice, call me names, etc.)" You will be hearing a lot about Super Hero Bear from your child. Here are some cues that you can use to encourage your child to talk about his feelings.

> Mad. You are mad at me! Tell me you feel mad right now.
> You can say you are angry. You may not yell at me or call me names.
> Stop and think. Use your words. Tell Mary how you feel.
> What can you say to him? How can you take care of yourself?
> Fantastic! You are a share-your-feelings kind of kid.

Super Hero Bear teaches adults positive cues to say when children get in trouble or are upset. Here are some examples of cues you can use at home:

> Chill out. Be cool. Get in control.
> Breathe, breathe, breathe three times and get your control.
> Tell yourself, "I am in charge of my body."
> Figure out what to do. Stop and think. You can do it.
> Use your words, not your fists!
> Tell your hands, "Keep to yourself if you want to have friends."
> Make a good choice. Use your words when you are angry.

Super Hero Bear encourages children to use their "Helper Words" to remind themselves positive things they can do when they are upset. Here are some Helper Words that children learn to problem solve and take responsibility for their actions:

> I use my Helper Words to help solve my problems.
> I tell myself to slow down when things go wrong.
> I use my words and say how I feel.
> I'll cool off by breathing two times for peace.
> I tell myself, "I can do this. I'll keep working and figure it out."

I am Many Parts—Jungian Psychology Techniques

From Carl Jung, we get the concept of the subparts of the personality. Children catch on quickly about their different parts. We will be learning about some of the different parts of the personality: The Sad Part, The Mad Part, The Trouble Part, The Baby Part, The Happy Part and The Special and Loved Part. You will hear your child talk about his "mads, sads, bads and scads" (a made up word for being scared).

Super Hero Bear teaches the children about the many parts that are inside of them. By learning about their mad, sad and trouble parts and the bad feelings inside them, the children learn to take responsibility for their behavior. They learn to let go of the overall label of "I AM BAD!" which decreases self-esteem causing them to act out in a self-fulfilling way. The lesson plans teach children to "own" their acting-out behaviors and make better choices in the future. The activities emphasize taking responsibility for one's actions and handling inner emotional distress.

The Emotional Freedom Technique Helps Release Unhappy Feelings

It is not enough to learn to share feelings. Children need ways to release their strong emotions. The Emotional Freedom Technique (EFT) is a new tool to help people accept and release their negative emotions. EFT is the quickest way to help you let go of feelings that bother you. It is a fast relaxation procedure that breaks into worry and stress. EFT will help your child learn the important skills of Emotional Intelligence to pave their way for a happier life. EFT can remind your child that he is in charge of his feelings and behavior. EFT gives your child choices so that he can make things better for himself.

Have you ever rubbed your head when you had a headache? Have you hugged yourself really tight when you were upset? Or pushed hard between your eyebrows or rubbed your temples when you were stressed or worried? People rub their bodies when they are stressed to get relief. That's why a massage feels good. Rubbing or tapping to put pressure on your body, so that you will feel better, is called acupressure.

Self-soothing includes all the ways that you take care of yourself when you are upset and stressed. Children need to learn techniques of self-soothing so they do not seek out detrimental things like alcohol and drugs when they get older. EFT is a soothing technique. Tapping while you think about what upsets you helps smooth out the too-much and too-little energy places. You poke on those emotional bumps and bruises and your energy starts flowing smoothly; then you feel much better.

EFT starts with stating the problem and then saying something positive about yourself. Admitting you have a problem helps you "own" it. Reminding yourself that you are a good person even though you have a problem helps you forgive yourself, learn from the mistake and do better next time. Having a good conscience, forgiving yourself for your mistakes and learning from those mistakes increases self-esteem. So EFT gets your child to take responsibility for his mistake and strive to do better next time!

EFT helps reduce stress and upsets that create acting out behavior in children. As we work thought these lesson plans on Emotional Intelligence, you will notice your child start to change and being more contented and less disruptive at home. You will observe that your child has fewer mood swings and is less demanding for material objects.

You can read more about The Emotional Freedom Technique at www.emofree.com or in Lynne Namka's book *Goodbye Ouchies and Grouchies, Hello Happy Feelings: EFT for Kids of All Ages.* See the AngriesOut web site at www.AngriesOut.com for other ideas on anger management for the whole family.

What You Can Do to Help!

Talk to your child each day about what he is learning about his feelings. Ask him what Super Hero Bear had to say. Review the pages and pictures that your child brings home. Encourage him to share his feelings at home. You can help your children develop positive self-esteem by validating their feelings. When you share your own upset feelings, you model a valued skill that will help children learn to take care of themselves. Become a "*Share your feelings family!*"

We will be making Super Hero Bears at school. Find an old teddy bear or buy an inexpensive one (some can be found for about a dollar) at a discount or thrift store for your child to bring to school. If you have extra teddy bears at home, we could use them for our project.

Learn the Emotional Freedom Technique to use on yourself when you are upset. It is the easiest tool to use to teach your child Emotional Intelligence. Use EFT when your child is distressed or angry to release unhappy feelings. And remember to do EFT daily yourself and be a "*Share-your-feelings kind of person!*"

Developing Emotional Intelligence in Your Family

Summarized from the book, *The Relationship Cure:*
A 5 Step Guide for Building Better Connections with Family, Friends, and Lovers
by John M. Gottman with Joan DeClaire

Dr. John M. Gottman and his wife Dr. Julie Schwartz-Gottman are the world's foremost researchers in understanding relationships. They invite couples to come into their research laboratory and talk and argue about challenging topics of their choice. They wire the couples up to sensory data machines and analyze the videotapes frame by frame to understand the complexities of human interaction. They found that there are basic verbal reactions that bond people together and cement relationships. They identified the ways that people use to try to gain attention and love. These skills of bidding for and responding to requests for attention are important components of Emotional Intelligence.

Positive bids are words, questions, gestures, looks, and ways of touching that reach out to another person to interact, "I want to be closer to you." The emotional needs that are met by bids includes 1) to be included, 2) to have a sense of control over their lives and 3) to be liked. Learning to make positive emotional bids is an important life skill of Emotional Intelligence, which will enhance the quality of your relationships with others.

Parents Teach Children to Deal with Feelings and Respond to Bids

Emotional bids are learned in infancy when the child cries and the parents respond either with attention, irritability or disinterest. The parent models the learned skill of validating the child by paying positive attention to him. The child practices his own emotional bidding first with family and then making and maintaining friends. Some children are quite adept at learning and reading social cues in relationships. Failure to learn the appropriate connecting skills typically results in non-nurturing friendships and later in failure in marriage and divorce.

Ways That Families Deal With Feelings That Increase Positive Bidding

1. **Emotional Coaching**: accepting feelings and helping the child problem solve the issue.

   You can get angry, but you must not yell at me. Talk to me about what upsets you.
   I know you feel scared. What can you do to take care of these feelings?
   When you are angry, you can draw a picture of your feelings.
   Let's talk about what you are feeling, and we can figure out what to do.

2. **Laissez-faire**: These parents acknowledge the feelings, but let the situation pass without problem solving. They typically do not have the skills to help the child work through upset feelings or are too busy with other things.

   You are feeling sad right now.
   I can tell that you are angry with me.
   I understand how you feel.

3. **Dismissing Feelings**: This includes silence or disparaging the child for having feelings. Fears are minimized and tears are ignored so the child learns to ignore his own feelings to fit into the family.

   Shame on you for being afraid. You are a big boy.
   If you don't stop crying, I'll give you something to cry about.

Cheer up. Put a smile on your face and get on with it.
You shouldn't feel that way.

4. **Disapproving of Emotions**: Parents scold and reprimand the children with shame statements and put-downs. The children learn to feel embarrassment about having feelings, hide them and discount them.

Oh stop your whining and crying. Grow up!
Ha. Ha. Look at the little crybaby.
What is the matter with you now? Do I need to give you something to cry about?

Gottman describes the type of family philosophy of dealing with feelings that work the best. He discusses how parents can demonstrate Emotional Intelligence to their children.

"In our two ten-year studies of more than one hundred families, the answer is clear. Families that create emotion-coaching environments fare much better than families that are dismissing, disapproving or have a laissez-faire attitude towards emotions. Couples who accept, respect and honor each other's feelings are less likely to divorce. Their children tend to do better over the years as well.

Because these emotional-coaching families create environments that help children regulate their feelings, their children can concentrate better than the kids in the other groups. They get better grades in school. They have fewer behavior problems and they get along better with their peers. Lab results show that they have fewer stress-related hormones in their bloodstreams and that over time, they suffer from fewer minor health problems like coughs and colds."

Ways People React to Bids for Connection

The opportunity for emotional connection is possible every time we engage in a conversation. Gottman's concept is simple. When we talk to people there is a possibility of three outcomes from the other person:

1.   To come closer (Turning Toward)
2.   To go further way (Turning Away)
3.   To stay at a neutral place.

Gottman found that happily married couples bid for connection often. They turn towards each other and bid with interest, smiles, humor and shared meanings. They develop a reciprocal interest-sharing kind of relationship. Gottman noted that some people consistently look for the wrong doings of their partners and then find it. Looking for the worst and then commenting on it can be a bad habit. Critical, judgmental people are usually met with Turning Away or Turning Against responses.

Turning Away Responses to Bids for Attention

Common Turning Away obstacles to connection in relationships include:

- Passive, noncommittal responses
- Preoccupied, ignoring responses
- Disregarding responses
- Interrupting and changing the subject

Turning Against Responses to Bids for Attention

The Turning Against responses that were negative and angry included:

- Belligerent responses such picking a fight.
- Wanting to debate and disagree.
- Domineering responses included attempts to control and to get the other person to back off.
- Critical responses such as blaming and judgments made about the other person.
- Defensive responses such as relinquishing responsibility by saying, "It's not my fault."
- Turning Away or attack are subtle ways of saying "I don't care to be bothered by you."
- Feelings of loss and disappointment bring trouble to a relationship.

You get what you put out. The Turning Away From and the Turning Against responses creates hurt, anxiety, disappointment and discouragement. These negative feelings then affect the quality of the relationship and create distrust and distancing. It is important for families to develop a "positive emotional bank account" filled with positive bidding and returned interest on their investment of the practice of seeing the good in things.

The Flooding of Stress Related Hormones Sends Fights Spinning Out of Control

Temper! Temper! The "fight or flight" response is a reaction to stress left over from our cave-man days. Flooding happens in people who become angry quickly. Hormones flood in to prepare the person to take care of himself in threatening situations. Adrenalin courses through the bloodstream to prepare for action. Physical signs of flooding are feeling energized, feeling hot, shallow breathing, and a pounding heart and muscle tension.

Unfortunately, common sense is thrown out the window when you become flooded. You say things you do not mean. Ugly words are tossed out. You shut off listening to your partner and sometimes go for the jugular vein. The over-excited behaviors that accompany flooding are you at your worst. Loud voices and rude behavior during an argument create even more conflict in the relationship, and the problem does not get worked out.

Dealing with the stress hormones during confrontation is another skill of Emotional Intelligence. You are always responsible for your anger. Abrupt leavings when you are angry without an explanation are not helpful. Leaving with sarcastic remarks can be damaging to the relationship.

Time outs to calm yourself and bring you back to your right mind are the recommendations given to people whose hormones get activated. Time outs can be established in advance with the purpose of helping the relationship. They can be stated as "For the good of the relationship, if my anger gets out of control, I need to go calm myself down. I'll go cool off then we can talk further." This contract should be set ahead of time so that both parties know that Time Outs are not meant as a rejection ploy, but done in the best interests of both.

So, if you feel your temper rising during a disagreement, ask to be excused and leave to get your strong feelings under control. Model for your children taking a time out and going to your room by saying, "I'm just too upset right now. I'm going to go take care of my hot feelings."

You need to agree to return to the discussion and not just sweep the unresolved issue unresolved. No fair going away and then coming back with fresh arguments as to why you are right—that only throws fuel on the fire! Come back when you are ready to compromise. Remember, people have different amounts of time that they require to calm themselves before they can return and discuss the issue in a quieter, calmer manner.

Fear of Fighting: Avoiding the Confrontation You Need to Hear

Some families are conflict avoidant. Refusing to discuss problems creates feelings of frustration, and builds up resentment in the partner who seeks closure. Avoidance of problem solving and sweeping problems under the rug sometimes results in even bigger blow-ups.

Sometimes it is not the right time to talk about a problem. Sometimes one partner refuses to discuss the problem. Little problems do need to be addressed before they grow into big ones. Gottman noticed three ways of dealing with conflict when one partner did not want to talk"

1. Attack the person and defend the self (You pay for this by the other person shutting down eventually.)
2. Avoid, deny or minimize when there is a problem (You pay for this because the other person remains angry. Anger builds up, as there is no escape valve to release it.)
3. Disclose feelings and make a connection. (If the time for talking out the problem is not appropriate, make a date to talk at a better time.)

Dealing with high emotional arousal is another skill of Emotional Intelligence. The nervous stomach, shortness of breath, fear reaction, etc. that conflict-avoidant people have can be addressed through relaxation techniques, which can be learned from most therapists. You can learn to stay to quell these physiological reactions to threat. The Emotional Freedom Technique can help you decrease and release feelings of distress.

Practice Emotional Bidding and Responses to Create a Happy Family

The moral of Gottman's research? Show interest in what your family members say and you will build up big dividends in your relationship. How you respond to your child's or partner's bids for attention will affect the quality of your relationship.

Making positive emotional bids and responding to them will increase the loving behavior in your household. Look for the good in the people in your family and make it known. Say what you like out loud and clear and you will get more of it.

The Emotional Freedom Technique

and

Lesson Plans for Teaching

Emotional Freedom

The Emotional Freedom Technique

From the book, *Goodbye Ouchies and Grouchies, Hello Happy Feelings: EFT for Kids of All Ages*

Problems are meant to be solved. You can become a problem solver with The Emotional Freedom Technique. Think of your problem. An unhappy feeling might pop up. Is your feeling sad, bad, mad, hurt, disappointed, frustrated, stubborn, or jealous? Give your feeling a name and feel it for a moment.

Remember, feelings are meant to be felt. That is why they are called feelings. Can't find your feelings? They are hiding out from you somewhere deep down inside. Think about them. They may decide to stop playing hide and seek. Ask yourself "Am I sad, mad, or feeling bad? Am I scared or confused?" Your feeling may pop up and join you later.

Say the problem and Tap on the outside of one hand down from your pinkie finger with the fingers of your other hand. This is called the Karate Chop. Think about your problem. Name the problem or the feeling that bothers you. Take a big breath and make it go way down to your belly. Then let your breath out slowly. Say your problem and say something good about yourself. This is called the Start Up Statement. Say anything positive. It doesn't matter what you say. Anything great you say will do. Make it REALLY positive.

Take a big breath and blow it out. Think of your problem and tap gently with both hands on these points of your body:

1. Between the inside of your eyebrows with your fingers.

2. Outside the corners of your eyes.

3. Under your eyes on your cheekbones.

4. Under your nose.

5. Under your bottom lip.

6. On your chest, just below your throat outside your collarbones.

7. Go straight down several inches and tap on your rib cage just above the last rib.

8. Below your armpit on the side of your body down several inches—like you are a funky chicken flapping his wings!

Don't worry if you don't get the exact point for tapping. Just tap! If you find a spot that's tender, give it special attention. Tap and breathe into it until your problem gets smaller or goes away.

Take a big belly breath and blow your problem out. Think of your problem again. Stretch your hands out to show how you feel about your problem now. Is your problem still as big? Sometimes your problem goes away. Sometimes the problem may still be there, but you feel differently about it.

Do you still have some of your problem? Say a different thing about your feelings or problem this time. Remember to say something good about yourself. Do the tapping again. Pick your problem apart. Keep thinking about the problem and tapping until you feel calm and your problem isn't important. Tap until your problem doesn't matter so much any more. Some boys and girls start out with their problem as big as the room and end up with it being a tiny problem. Do EFT on any thing that upsets you that comes up. Keep doing it until you feel better. Remember, you can't do it wrong. Just do it!

Super Hero Bear to the Rescue!

Objective: To learn to express feelings.

Materials: Super Hero Bear

Activity: Super Hero Bear Helps Me Share Feelings: Introduce the Super Hero Bear by flying him through the air with a flourish and humming a snatch of music from the William Tell Overture and say "Da ta da da! Super Bear to the rescue!"

Dialogue: "Fly" Super Hero Bear in from behind your back and say, "Do you have a problem? Super Hero Bear to the rescue! Super Hero Bear knows about problems and wants you to share your feelings. He will help you learn to work out your bad feelings. Everybody has some bad feelings once in a while. There is nothing as bad as hurting inside and not being able to talk about it. Here are some feelings your might have: bad, sad, mad, glad and scad (a made up word for scared.) Tell us about your feelings."

Have the Super Hero Bear talk sympathetically to the children using these phrases that encourage sharing of feelings. Have Super Hero Bear "say" these phrases to the children.

       Tell me how you feel...
       Are you feeling mad right now? Use your feeling words.
       I feel sad when you tell me _____. How do you feel?
       I like it when you share your mad feelings with me...
       Sharing feelings gets the mad out.
       You certainly know how to share your feelings.
       I'm proud of you. You let those feelings out.
       Check and see. How do you feel?
       I think there might be another feeling in there. Look and see what else is there.
       Don't you feel good now that you've let those bad feelings out?
       Awesome! You can talk out those feelings!
       Let's do a feeling check. Tell me...

Reflect the child's words back to her stating the feeling behind the experience: "You felt really sad when your sister told on you." Usually children correct you if you get it wrong. If a child says something that is too private for the group, ask her to save those feelings just for the two of you later or refer her to the guidance counselor if appropriate.

Cues
       Use your words. Use your firm, fair words.
       Stop and think. What do you need to say?
       Tell him, don't hit him, and tell him about it. Work it out with him.
       Tell _____ how you feel when he does that. Remember when you are hurting inside, talk about it.

Helper Words for Children
       I can use my Helper Words to help me get my feelings out.
       When I feel threatened, I'll tell myself, "Go ahead and talk about it."
       I tell myself, "I feel good about working this out." Helper Words make me powerful.

Tips for parents and teachers: Super Hero Bear is a combination of teacher/coach/cheerleader who teaches statements of appropriate choice, discernment and positive self-esteem to children. Kids love the Super Hero Bear concept and will begin saying his statements to each other. Have the children give each other advice via the Super Hero Bear. Kids need to hear these positive phrases over and over again in order to learn to express their feelings. Repetition is the best way to learn a new skill.

The Okays About Feelings For Kids of All Ages:

It is okay for you to feel any way you feel.

It is okay for your feelings to change.

It is okay to feel sad and angry when you have been hurt.

It is okay to feel confused if you don't understand.

It is okay to feel scary inside.

It is okay to cry when you are hurting.

It is okay to talk about your unhappy feelings.

It is okay to ask for help.

It is okay to ask for a hug or to be held.

It is okay to let bad feelings go.

It is okay for you to take care of yourself.

It is okay for you to feel happy again.

It is most certainly okay for you to be yourself.

It is okay to be who you are.

Helper Words Help Me Feel Good

Objective: To learn Helper Words to increase attention to task.

Materials: Super Hero Bear

Activity: <u>Super Hero Bear Talk Helps Me Be Responsible</u>: Super Hero Bear is a cool, hip guy who encourages children to create peaceful solutions to problems. Use him to encourage the children to be responsible for gaining control over their actions. Teach these Helper Words to help children stop their own misbehavior. Talk to the children about the positive attributes of self-control.

<u>Super Hero Bear Dialogue</u>: "People who are in control of their own body can feel good about themselves. They have learned to say Helper Words to themselves to stop themselves when they are about to get in trouble. Helper Words help us remember how to take care of ourselves when things get tough."

You can put my Helper Words in your brain to help you out. Helper Words give you ideas of things to do when things go wrong. They help you when you feel threatened or angry. You can use Helper Words to help yourself. Here are some of my best Helper Words:

> I stop and think. I take care of myself.
> I'll make a good choice. I feel good about being in charge.
> I use Helper Words to feel good about myself.
> I can use my words to help me get the job done.
> I talk to myself when I need help. I will always be there for myself.
> I stop myself from doing things which get me in trouble.

Have the children repeat the Helper Words along with Super Hero Bear several times. Give several examples of stressful situations. Ask the children what they could say to help themselves in these challenging situations.

> You are trying to do your homework and keep making mistakes.
> The sand castle you are building keeps caving in.
> Mom says you have to clean your room, but you don't want to.
> Your friend wants you to play, but you promised your dad you would rake the yard.
> You are carrying a huge bunch of stuff and keep dropping it.
> You are angry because you have to wash the dishes.
> You are working on some problems and they are really hard.

<u>EFT Tapping Phrases</u>
Even though this work is hard to do, I keep going.
Even though it's hard for me to keep my attention on my work, I forgive myself.
Even though I get mad when things go wrong, I'm still a good kid.

<u>Tips for parents and teachers</u>: All of the Super Hero Bear statements serve as cues for teachers. Other than a pet, Super Hero Bear may be the closest thing to unconditional love that some children may have in their life. He provides a voice of reason and other alternatives to some of the messages they get in other settings. Super Hero Bear is a Master Teacher whose positive phrases can be a continual force for change in young children's lives.

Some children do not have a vocabulary for emotions. Label the emotions for the young child who is not yet talking or the child who has repressed his feelings. For example say, "Mad, you look like you are feeling mad right now. Say it: Mad, I feel mad." This statement gives the child a label for what is going on internally so that he can learn to express his feelings verbally instead of through acting out and temper tantrums. It also gives him permission to be angry.

Cues to Help Hurt and Angry Children Talk About Feelings

Make a good choice. Stop and think. Let's have a feeling check.

What are you feeling right now? Sad, bad, glad, mad and scad (Southern talk for scared!)

Check your insides and tell me how you feel.

Use your words. Use your words, not your fists. Tell him how you feel.

You are not a bad kid; you have strong feelings that you need to understand.

It is okay to have uncomfortable emotions. If you talk about them, they go away.

Feelings help us learn about ourselves.

It is okay to be upset, frustrated, sad and angry if you express your feelings in ways that don't hurt others.

Use your words and talk about your angry feelings.

Is there hurt under your anger?

You can't make the other person change with your words, but you feel good because you spoke up for yourself.

Find someone safe to talk to. Take care of yourself. Get those feelings out!

We can share feelings here and work it out.

Remember to share your feelings when you are upset. Who can you share with?

We are a *"talking-it-out kind of group/class/family."*

We are a *"share-your-feelings kind of group/class/family."*

Tips for parents and teachers: Positive cues about sharing feelings give an immediate alternative response to the upset or misbehaving child. These key phrases do not belittle or shame the child. They help him save face by showing him as to what he can do to take care of himself. They remind him to make a responsible choice to feel good about himself. They work! The constant repetition of these cues helps the child incorporate them into his belief system. Add these cues gradually to your repertoire. Practice one cue for several days until you hear yourself saying it automatically in response to specific children's behavior. Post several cues around your room to assist you in learning.

I Can Share My Feelings

Objective: To learn to express feelings appropriately

Materials: Super Hero Bear

Activity: Have Super Hero Bear talk to the Children: Super Bear talks about using the "I feel ____ formula." "You can learn to use your words when you are upset with others or yourself. You can say "I feel _____ when you _____." to get your feelings out. You can say, "I feel upset with myself when _____."

Sharing your feelings with strong, firm words helps you take your power. Some people can hear your feelings. Some families are just beginning to learn to share feelings. Many of your parents did not learn this skill when they were young. You may want to teach your parents about this. Some people are not comfortable talking about their feelings. Some parents will learn; some will not. You can feel good about saying how you feel with other people even if your family does not talk about their feelings.

The purpose of sharing feelings is to get them out of you so they don't get stuck. Sharing feelings will NOT make the other person do what you want. You still have to mind your parents and do what they expect you to do even though you share your feelings!"

You may hear the children start to use appropriate feeling statements spontaneously. Encourage them to express all emotions by making it safe when they do so. Reinforce children who use appropriate expression of anger by saying, "Thanks for sharing your feelings. Now that you have shared them, you can take care of them by breathing or tapping them out."

Activity: Stop being the Referee: When children come to you to tell of conflict, tell them to use their firm, fair words and work it out with the other person. Tell them that you believe in their ability to be fair and work out their issue with each other. Ask them to come back to report to you how they have worked it out. Given a few guidelines, children can be remarkably effective at working out their own problems.

Cues When Children Are In Conflict or Feeling Bad
    What are your feeling right now?
    What could the two of you agree on?
    What could you do to take care of yourself right now?
    Remember sharing feelings makes you feel good. Its purpose is not to change the other person.
    Use your words. Your words can help you feel better about yourself.
    You need to go take care of your bad feelings. Figure out how to let them go.
    Shake them out. Shake out those uncomfortable feelings. You can do it. Shake them out.

EFT Tapping Phrases
    Even though it is hard for me to share my feelings, I'm an awesome kid.
    Even though I don't feel good about some of my feelings, I choose to get them out.
    Even though sharing feelings is scary, I take care of myself.
    Even though it is hard for me to stand up and say what I mean, I forgive myself.

Tips for parents and teachers: In times of conflict, positive adult cues can empower the distraught child. The use of a correctly phrased cue after disruptive or unwelcome behavior is an important tool that teachers have in their arsenal of skills. Learning these cues takes minimal effort and gives you a thousand-fold return on your investment of time. The direct message to the child is that you believe in his ability to get his act together plus giving a minimum of information how he might take care of himself. A positive message about how to act appropriately to take care of himself can be effective for the child who is hurting. The message comes through again and again--you believe in his ability to work things out. This ties into the self-fulfilling prophecy. "Someone believes in me so I must have what it takes to work out the threatening situation!"

ANGRY FEELINGS ARE A PART OF LIFE

IT'S OK TO BE MAD
IF YOU ARE FIRM AND FAIR ABOUT IT

Super Hero Bear Helps Me Solve Problems

Objective: To learn to problem solve.

Materials: Super Hero Bear

Activity: Problem Solving With Super Hero Bear: Have the Super Hero Bear use open-ended questions to encourage the children to express their feelings and figure things out for themselves. Open-ended questions start with "who, why and what." Encourage the children to process their conflicts and come up with alternative solutions to aggression. Praise them for thinking hard and coming up with new ideas. Use these processing phrases to stimulate taking responsibility for problem solving around conflict. Have Super Hero Bear show excitement when children come up with original thinking. Have the children draw a picture on the following page.

Here are some open-ended questions for Super Hero Bear to use to get the children talking about problem solving:

Amael felt angry when Jerry hit him without any reason. What could he do?
Did anyone ever have something like this happen? Tell us about it.
What do you think might have happened if you had _____?
What's another way this could be handled?
What else could you do?
What do you feel when a big kid picks on you. What do you do?
Who can tell about feeling angry when someone hurt you?
Yes, you must really feel sad and hurt about that. Has anyone else felt like this?
How do you feel when a grownup yells at you? What do you do?
What's another thing you could have done? Some other things?
What will you do next time someone yells at you?
How do you show the folks at your house that you are angry? What is another way?

Show sympathy for the children as they describe things that hurt them. You need not try to solve all of their problems. If you do not know what to say to a child say, "I'm sorry that happened to you. Thank you for sharing with us." Sometimes a child's talking about a bad experience with a caring listener helps him.

Activity: Teach self-correction instead of adult correction: Work yourself out of constant disciplining children. Instead of correcting a child, use these phrases to ask him to correct himself!

Tell yourself, "I'll get my control. Make a good choice."
Remember to say, "I am in control of what I say and do."
Remind yourself to make your hands friendly to others.
Tell your hands to "Keep to yourself." Say, "I have friendly hands."
Remember to say, "I'll ask before I touch. I ask_____ if I can touch her arm. I ask first."
Give yourself a hug and say, "I'll do something that makes me feel good."

EFT Tapping Phrases
Even though I did something wrong, I am learning to be a better person.
Even though I want to hurt someone, I keep my control.
Even though I'm angry about _____, I love and forgive myself.
Even though I have a humongous problem, I can problem solve it!

I put Super Hero Bear words in my brain.

He helps me be in charge of my behavior.

I tell my hands "Keep to yourself." I have friendly hands.

I tell myself, "No big deal. Just deal with this."

I say, "Chill out. I'll cool myself down about this. I'm cool."

I remind myself, "Let it go. This is not worth getting upset about."

I Use Helper Words to do a Better Job!

<u>Objective</u>:   To learn self-reinforcing statements to increase attention to the task.

<u>Materials</u>:   Super Hero Bear.

<u>Activity</u>:   <u>I Put Super Hero Bear Words in My Brain!</u>: Use the Super Hero Bear to teach children self-reinforcing phrases. Super Hero Bear is a wise bear who knows that adults will not be around in most situations to give the child external reinforcement. He provides a way to internalize positive phrases within the child by saying "Tell yourself____. The child is taught to reinforce his own effort so he won't be dependent upon adults. Super Hero Bear links positive Helper Words with feeling happy so that children associate feeling good with learning.

Ask the children which Helper Words they want to put in their brain. Emphasize how the body feels relaxed and happy when positive words are used. Get the children to check in with their body to strengthen their knowledge of how their body feels when they use positive statements.

> Awesome! Tell yourself, "Awesome!"
> You've got it. Give yourself five!
> Whoa! That's a fantastic choice. Say "Fantastic!"
> You've got what it takes to think for yourself. Give yourself a high five!
> You are a great problem-solver. Tell yourself, "I can solve problems."
> Check your tummy. Don't you feel good inside when you work hard? Say, "I can get it!"
> Cool! You got your control back. Tell yourself, "I'm in charge here. I can chill out."
> Fantastic!" You took your own time-out. Say, "I'm the boss of my own feelings."
> Give yourself a big pat on the back.
> Great sharing of feelings! Tell yourself how good you feel when you get the feelings out.
> Hey, you are pretty good at this. Remember to tell yourself "I'm good at this?"
> Say it, "All right! Way to go!!!"

Write out favorite reinforcing Helper Words statements and post them around the room. Write out each child's statement of choice to take home. Choose one statements as the password of the day and saturate the children with it. Ask the children to reinforce their learning by reminding each other of the positive Helper Words. Have Super Hero Bear keep a secret ear out to listen for children who are using self-reinforcing statements and those who give positive statements to reinforce their classmates.

<u>Activity</u>:   <u>Adult Modeling</u>: Use the "I feel ____ formula" yourself, to model appropriate ways to express uncomfortable feelings to the children several times during the day. As their parent or teacher, give yourself permission to talk your stress out loud instead of repressing it to the point where it comes out in inappropriate ways. Using "I" messages to express your own feelings will give the children a strong useful model of what they can do to take care of their feelings:

> I feel frustrated when you interrupt the group.
> I feel angry when I try to talk and your voices are so loud that I can't be heard.
> When I see you hit yourself in the head, I feel sad.
> I'm feeling upset now. I'll say how I feel before I get to my boiling over point.

<u>EFT Tapping Phrases</u>
> Even though I goof up sometimes, I still like myself.
> Even though I forget what to do, I use Helper Words to figure it out.

Yes I Can Because I Think I Can!

Objective: To learn Helper Words effort statements to motivate performance.

Materials: Book—*The Little Red Engine* (available in most libraries) and Super Hero Bear.

Activity: Read *The Little Red Engine*: Emphasize how the engine had to talk himself through a tough task. Repeat the refrain, "I think I can, I know I can!" several times. Tie in the idea of breathing deeply to doing well on a task. The Little Engine needed fuel to get up the mountain. Our body's fuel is food, water and oxygen which we get from breathing.

Use Super Hero Bear to act as a motivator for children who are passive and caught in the "I can't" pattern of behavior. Have Super Hero Bear emphasize that he believes in the children's ability to take care of themselves. Have him show the children how to break into whatever they are doing that doesn't work and problem solve the situation. Have Super Hero Bear teach the children to use self-reinforcing statements.

> Remember to be your own cheerleader. Tell yourself, "I can do it."
> Remember the Little Red Engine -- "I know I can, I know I can..."
> Remind yourself -- "I'll try harder, I'll get it."
> Tell yourself, "I'll try it a different way -- I'll get it."
> Say to yourself, "It's tough, but I can take it. With hard work, I'll figure it out."
> I feel good when I work hard. I'll pat myself on the back.

Children who are unmotivated to do their work could earn the right to have Super Hero Bear sit on their desk by finishing a prescribed amount of their schoolwork. Have the child write out the phrases that he wants to use to remind himself about getting his work done. Post these phrases on his desk. Walk by his desk and see if you can "catch" him saying the positive self-talk statements out loud. Write a contract with the child giving him a few minutes of playing with the Super Hero Bear after the work is done. Some children enjoy just playing with Super Hero Bear during free time, flying him around the room making positive statements!

Helper Words for Children:
I make myself feel good by saying positive things to myself.
Learning is fun when I am my own cheerleader.
I'll put Super Hero Bear words in my own brain.

EFT Tapping Phrases
Even though I tell myself "I can't" at times, I keep on trying.
Even though I don't want to do my work, I do it anyway.
Even though I shut myself down by thinking "I can't" I try harder.

Tips for parents and teachers: The research shows that failure on a task divides children into two camps--the Mastery Oriented and the Learned Helplessness. Up until the time of failure, the children from the two groups are pretty much the same. However, once they hit a snag, children either put their energy into solving the task or avoiding it. The difference between the two groups is the internal cognitions they make or WHAT THEY SECRETLY TELL THEMSELVES!

Children who display Learned Helplessness give up and say things like "This is too hard. I never was good at this. I hate doing this task. I wonder what we are going to have for supper. Maybe I'll go out and play after school. Boring. This is BORING!" All these internal thoughts focus the child's attention away from the task. Energy goes into avoidance of the task. Mastery Oriented children, on the other hand, direct all their energy into problem solving. They have internal thoughts like "Oh boy, this is fun. This is a challenge. I'll keep going and I'll get it. Maybe if I try it this way, I'll figure it out. I'll keep trying. I can get it." They have learned to psych themselves up to complete the task.

For more information, see Martin Seligman's book "*The Optimistic Child: A Proven Program to Safeguard Children from Depression and Build Lifelong Resistance.*"

The I Can't Part Keeps Me from Getting the Job Done

Objective: To learn how attitude affects task performance.

Materials: Stuffed animals brought by the children from home.

Activity: The I Can't I Can Contest: Have a contest with the children to have them bring in several stuffed animals that could represent the I Can't or I Don't Want To Part. Narrow the animal candidates down to several and have the children vote on which stuffed animal is typical of their resistance to do things they do not want to do. Have the children discuss the situations where the foot-dragging part comes out and takes over. Rename this part the Slow To Get Started But I'm Going To Get There Part! Encourage the children to find their Helper Words fast when they feel the I Can't Part coming out.

Have the children list the internal statements that they tell themselves which interfere with completing a task. Call this list "Things I Tell Myself To Get Out of Work." Approach this topic in a humorous way, sharing some of your own negative and critical statements that you would like to change in yourself. Acknowledge that everyone has a bit of this part and that it is normal to not want to do every thing. Discuss how giving in to negative internal statements on a regular basis sets the stage for failure. Show the children that you get what you put into things--your energy can go into getting out of work OR it can go into getting the job done making time available to do other things.

Typical Things I Tell Myself To Get Out of Work   (This is also the Beat Yourself Up List!)
    This is too hard. I never was any good at ____. I'm stupid.
    Why do I have to do this dumb old thing? It's not fair.
    I'll put it off until later.
    I don't like ____. I don't want to do this. I can't get it.
    Any distraction statement such as thinking about recess, after school, fantasies, etc.

Have the children identify which tasks or chores that they find hard to do. Have each child draw a four panel cartoon of this part showing how negative self-statements cause him to get down on himself, prolong his agony and even give up on the task. Have the children generate Super Hero Bear Helper Words, which they can use to break into their negative mind set. Have the children draw a picture on the following page.

Helper Words for Children
    I tell myself I'll get it and I do. I use Helper Words to keep me working hard.
    Super Hero Bear and I can figure it out
    I think I can. I know I can!
    Helper Words help me keep my mind on what I do.
    I'll breathe deeply and let go of my "Can'ts!"
    I'll use my Helper Words to feel good about myself. No more beating myself up!

EFT Tapping Phrases
    Even though I called myself stupid when the work was hard, I forgive myself.
    Even though I get myself all upset over doing my chores, I accept who I am.
    Even though I get bored when work gets hard, I give myself a pep talk with Helper Words.
    Even though I give my attention to other things instead of finishing my work, I love myself.
    Even though this work is hard, I tell myself to keep going and I'll get it.

Tips for parents and teachers: Learned Helplessness is the giving up on a task after failure due to internal negative feedback. Think about your own life. In what areas are you a victim of your negative thoughts? What are your "Can'ts?" In what areas are you your best cheerleader? Watch your thoughts and teach the children to watch theirs.

I put Super Hero Bear Helper Words
in my brain to help me solve problems.

I tell myself "I can do hard work."

Way to go! I can get this.
Super Hero Bear and I can figure this out
I think I can. I know I can!
I stop and think. I am smart. I'll get it!

The I Can and I Can't Contest

Objective: To learn that what we tell ourselves affects performance.

Activity: My Choice— I Can or Can't: Do an experiment by looking at the time and accuracy of a hard task (building a tower of blocks too high or completing a page of addition facts) under children's negative self-statement conditions and then after giving themselves a pep talk. "This is easy. I can do it." vs. "It's too hard. This is impossible." Children can become aware of how they handicap themselves down by giving in to internal negative self-statements.

Use Super Hero Bear to talk to a child who express frustration and failure often. Set up a dialogue between his "I Can't" part and his "I Can, Because I Think I Can" part to show the conflict that resistance causes.

Super Hero Bear Dialogue with Child who Role-Plays saying "I can't."
> I Can't"— I never was any good at this. Math is just too hard.
> I Can — Will you listen to yourself? What are you doing to yourself?
> I Can't — It's no use. These problems are just too hard.
> I Can — They will be hard if you tell yourself they are hard. What could you say differently to help yourself out?
> I Can't — But I'm stupid.
> I Can — Maybe your stupidity is just in what you say to yourself, not what you really are. Come on. Give yourself a chance. Use only loving, caring words with yourself. Don't beat yourself up. What Helper Words will you use?

Activity: Drawing Page: Have the children make a border for the page by writing Helper Words continuously around the edges of the page. Ask them to choose the phrases they want to put in their brain. Have them draw a picture of themselves being empowered with the help of their favorite Super Hero Bear and Helper Words.

Ways to Say, "You Can Do It Better!"
> You can learn from your mistakes!
> Keep working. It looks like you've almost got it.
> Tell yourself, "I'll try it a different way."
> You have almost got it. Keep trying. What can you say to yourself?

EFT Tapping Phrases
> Event though I made a mistake, I learn from it and move on.
> Even though I forgot and called myself a dummy, I know I am smart.
> Even though I'd rather goof off and be lazy, I keep at my work.
> Even though I feel stressed and want to give up, I tap on my stressful feelings.
> Even though I give up too easily at times, I deal with my bad feelings and keep working.

Tips for parents and teachers: Let Super Hero Bear and his positive Helper Words become the motivator and disciplinarian. A little time spent in making these cues part of your automatic response to children's disruptions will dramatically change your life! Things to remember in praising a child who is unmotivated:

1.   Recognize effort as well as accomplishment.
2.   Ask the child to judge her own effort and make discriminations as to which work is acceptable
3.   Believe in her ability to do her best.
4.   Get the child to praise her self. ("Tell yourself I did awesome work.")

I Am Many Parts: The Trouble Part

Objective: To learn about the Trouble Part.
                To talk about feelings and share unhappy experiences.

Materials: Stuffed animals representing Trouble Part and Super Hero Bear

Activity: Accepting the Trouble Part: Keep voice cheerful and matter of fact as you talk about the Trouble Part without judgment. Tell the children that we humans have many parts inside of us. Learning about our parts helps us understand ourselves. Talk about your own Trouble Part giving examples of how you got in trouble as a child.

Encourage the children to talk about their Trouble Part emphasizing their feelings that hide underneath getting in trouble. Remind the children that talking about these parts and the accompanying bad feelings helps let them go. Hold up the part that you introduce while you talk about it and then hand it to the child who volunteers to talk about that part of himself.

Dialogue: "Sometimes you do something and you feel really, really bad. Sometimes people tell you that you are bad when you do something wrong. You are not bad, but you may have a part in you that gets you in trouble. (Hold up the Trouble Part to demonstrate.) Our Trouble Part is our hands, feet or mouth. You may have a big Trouble Part or a little Trouble Part. He is always hanging around to get you in trouble. The Trouble Part comes out and then you get scolded. That Trouble Part gets you into hot water. Sometimes it acts out to get attention. Remember, you are not a bad kid but you haven't learned to get your Trouble Part under control yet. If you can find your Trouble Part, you can talk to it and get it to work with you."

Discussion Questions for Finding the Trouble Part
    What do you think, do you have a big, little or medium size Trouble Part?
    Stretch your hands out and show how big your Trouble Part is.
    What do your hands, feet or mouth do to get you in trouble?
    Tell about a time when you tried very hard to be good but got in trouble anyway?
    How do you feel when you get in trouble? What do you do then?
    How do you get attention? Does your way of getting attention sometimes make people angry?

What are some poor ways of getting adult attention? (Teasing, whining, helplessness, temper tantrums, victim talk, etc.)

After you model the Super Hero Bear talking to the Trouble part, hand the Super Hero Bear to a child and have her take the Super Hero Bear role talking to her own Trouble part. Be sympathetic to stories of pain and unhappiness. If appropriate, give information about what the child could have done differently in the situation so that he wouldn't get in trouble.

When a child becomes upset or angry, have the Super Hero Bear remind him to talk about his feelings. Super Hero Bear can suggest better choices next time the child is in a similar situation. Children will accept more information about their negative attitudes and behavior from the Super Hero Bear than they will from a moralizing adult. Have the Super Hero Bear talk to the Trouble Part, giving the child specific information about what he won't get in trouble in the future.

Super Hero Bear Comments When A Child's Trouble Part Comes Out
    Stop and think. Make a good choice.
    Does your mouth get you in trouble? Get it under control by taking a deep breath.
    Ask before you touch. Tell your hands to hold on until you ask for permission.
    You don't have to bring out your Trouble Part to get attention.
    What could you do besides teasing _____? What do you really want from him?

Making My Own Super Hero Bear

Objective: To learn Helper Words to stop the Trouble Part from acting out.
To find the bad feelings that hide under the Trouble Part.

Materials: Troubled Part and Super Hero Bear.

Activity: Super Hero Bear: Have each child bring a teddy bear to class to develop his or her own Super Hero Bear (Thrift stores have bears for 50 cents.) Make simple cape patterns of various sizes. Let the children make small capes out flashy material by cutting them out with pinking shears. Keep the bears on the children's' desks for a week. When a child asks your advice, ask them what Super Hero Bear might say.

Activity: I Act Out My Trouble Part: Role-playing is a good activity to get children to act out their Trouble Part. You may need to break the ice by acting out something you did wrong as a child and the consequences. Cast the children in the different roles (such as the upset parent, teacher, and principal) and give them their lines reflecting typical scenes where children get in trouble.

Dialogue: "Sometimes our mouth becomes the Trouble Part when we speak out when we are not supposed to or say something rude. We all have had times when our mouth really set us up for some terrible consequences. Right? Let's act out these two scenes:

"Okay, let's act it out using the mistake of talking out in class. Who wants to be the teacher? Who wants to act the part of the Trouble Part with the loud mouth? Who wants to be Super Hero Bear whispering in the loud mouth's ear reminding about the good choices that can be made? End the role playing by showing the positive ways of acting.

"This Trouble Part can't keep his hands to himself. Who wants to play the part of Joe who bothers others with his hands? Who wants to play the parts of being teased and bothered? Who wants to be Super Hero Bear and share some Helper Words? Let's set the stage. Everyone is working hard when Joe lets his Trouble Part out. Joe, how does your Trouble Part act out? Super Hero Bear, what do you say when Joe's Trouble Part comes out? How can you help him stop?"

Activity: Finding the Bad Feelings: Help the children find their bad feelings that are underneath their Trouble Part. Draw a picture of your own bad feelings. Hide the picture under your shirt or sweater. Dramatically pull the Bad Feelings out of yourself and show relief on your face to demonstrate letting them go. Toss them aside with flair into the trash basket! Have the children draw pictures about their own bad feelings. Have them pull their pictures out from under their shirt and throw them away.

Helper Words for Children
I am in charge of what I do. Super Hero Bear and I can figure this out.
I make good choices. Stop, look and listen before I act.
I use Helper Words to stop my hands/mouth/feet from getting me in trouble.
When I want attention, I ask for it. I know I won't always get it. That's how it is.

EFT Tapping Phrases
Even though I have a big Trouble Part, I tap on it every day.
Even though my hands get me in trouble, I love and forgive myself.
Even though I feel bad about doing things that upset others, I forgive myself.
Even though it is hard for me to keep my hands to myself, I'm still a good kid.

I Learn About My Mads

Objectives: To learn alternate responses to acting out when upset.
                     To learn to talk out angry feelings.

Materials: Mad Part and Bad Feelings Part

Activity: Mad Part: Tell the children that everyone has a Mad Part. Human beings get the mads now and then. The Mad Part feels irritable, crabby and grumpy and sometimes has a tantrum. Anger is normal and can be studied so that you can do it ways that do not hurt others or yourself.

Dialogue: "Anger is a feeling that everyone has. It's okay to have a Mad Part. Its okay to feel angry but you have to be thoughtful about letting it out. We have to be careful how we express anger so that we don't cause harm to others. The Mad Part in us comes out when someone hurts us or we don't get our way. Maybe your Mad Part came out when you tried to do something and it went all wrong. Some people with mad parts blow up and explode all of the time. Others go inside their shell and hide.

There are big mads such as being seriously hurt and little mads such as not getting your way. Your little Mad Part is frustration and irritability and the big Mad Part comes out as a temper tantrum and rage. Sometimes the Sad and Mad Part go together along with a Confused Part. Anger is a response to feeling hurt about something that happened to you. Hey, who is this hiding under the Mad Part? Hurt hides under the Mad Part! Hurt feelings usually hide deep down under the Mad Part

The mads stay inside getting angrier and angrier until you talk about what made you angry. Talking about the Mad Part makes it feel better. The mad feelings can go away when you talk about them. Sometimes there is a Sad Part hiding under the anger. Sometimes you feel mad and sad and hurt all at the same time. Most mads stick around until you talk about them. Remember, you don't need to hold on to your mads. You don't need to blow up or pout when you are upset. Use your words. Talk about it and feel better."

Ask the children to share their experiences about being angry. Hand each child the Mad Part and Bad Feelings Part as he talks about his feelings. Reflect back the frustration and anger that each child describes with empathetic statements such as "That must have really upset you. I bet you felt really bad inside."

Super Hero Bear Comments to the Mad Part: Fly the Super Hero Bear from around your back in with a fanfare (Da, ta, ta, da!) to talk to the Mad Part.
    Use your words, not your fists. Talk it out.
    Chill out. Be cool, dude. You can let go of your mads by deep breathing.
    Is this a big thing or a little thing? No big deal. You can blow this one off.
    Don't get all red and huffy about it. Use your words then you will feel better.
    It is okay to be mad if you are firm and fair about it.
    You don't have to be a crab. Don't go hide in your shell. Tell me about it.
    It is no fun to hang on to your mads. Shake them off. Talk them out!

EFT Tapping Phrases
    Even though I get mad easily, I'm still an okay kid.
    Even though I have a hot temper, I breathe and cool myself off.
    Even though I get upset over little things, I learn to chill myself out.
    Even though I get angry when people tease me, I tap and let it go.

Tips for parents and teachers: Somehow the use of the word "mads" and "bads" helps the children accept their anger and want to change their acting out behavior. By normalizing the emotions and making these less mystifying, children learn to handle their internal distress which is a major skill needed for Emotional Intelligence.

Use Your Words, Not Your Fists

Objective: To express anger in an appropriate way.

Activity: Song: (To the tune of "When You're Happy and You Know It, Clap Your Hands.")

              If you're angry and you know it, use your words!
              If you're angry and you know it, use your words!
              If you're angry and you know it,
              Then your body's going to show it,
              If you're angry and you know it, use your words!

              If you're angry and you know it, tell someone!
              If you're angry and you know it, tell someone.
              If you're angry and you know it,
              Then your body's going to show it,
              If you're angry and you know it, tell someone!

Activity: Role Playing: Encourage problem solving to deal with angry feelings and using words instead of fists. Set up role situations to practice this new skill of anger release. Model the incorrect and correct ways to act and ask the children to act out the different ways of dealing with a threatening situation. Choose some real life conflicts from your classroom after the children get the hang of saying the formula in pretend situations. Role Playing allows the child to gain mastery over a new skill in a non-threatening situation in a firm, fair voice.

Role Playing Examples

"Mary, pretend that you bump into Joe when he walks by. Joe, your job is to remember to use your words when you feel angry. What can you say to her to express your feelings? Remember to use your firm and fair words to take care of yourself.

"Gary, let's pretend that Jeff has just grabbed your ball. You can choose what to do: Hit him, tell the teacher or take care of it yourself. What would happen if you do each of these things?

"Shawn, pretend you struck out when playing softball. You are disappointed and angry. What could you do with your bad feelings?

"Laurie, remember a time when you were mad because your Math homework was so hard. Tell us what you could do instead of getting angry and yelling about the assignment? What could you do instead of getting mad at yourself or the teacher?

"Josie, pretend you are angry at your little brother who keeps bugging you. How can you keep your cool? What firm, fair words could you say to him? What bargain could you make with him?"

Helper Words
          I can problem solve when I'm angry. I can take care of myself. I can deal with this.
          I can keep my control. I can make a good choice.
          I'm big enough to listen to others when they tell me they are upset with me.

Tips for parents and teachers: The ability to express anger in a meaningful yet socially acceptable way when threatened is one of the highest-level social skills. Children as young as three years of age can learn to say the "I feel formula" when this phrase is taught and reinforced daily. Learning to express negative feelings appropriately prepares the child to empathize, another high level skill necessary for intimate relationship.

I AM A SPEAK-MY-FEELINGS
KIND OF PERSON!

MY FIRM AND FAIR WORDS MAKE ME POWERFUL

I USE MY WORDS TO TAKE CARE OF MYSELF.

Why And When We Get Angry

Objective: To understand the most common reasons people get angry.

Activity: Understand When You Get Angry. Explain to the children that anger is a normal emotion that people feel when they lose something important or their expectations are not met. Make a poster of these reasons and ask the children make their own copy. There can be more than one area of threat for an incident (for example your body and feelings are hurt.) Ask the children to give examples from their own lives of feeling strong emotions. As children express their feelings of hurt, disappointment and anger, point to the poster and ask to decide if the threat was to their body, property, etc.

Body: Someone hits, kicks or does physical harm to your body.

Property: Someone takes or breaks your belongings.

Values: Someone acts in ways that are inconsistent with what you believe such as honesty and respects for others. They lie, steal or hurt others.

Self Esteem: Someone discounts you, teases you or says something that is untrue or unfair about you. This brings up feeling of being unworthy. Anger can be used to help you stand up for yourself or anger is substituted to avoid the bad feeling of shame.

Guilt: You did something wrong and got angry when confronted to avoid responsibility or to get the other person to back off. Anger becomes a substitute feeling to ward off guilt and keeps you from taking responsibility for your misdeeds.

Unmet Expectations: You didn't get what you wanted and think it is unfair. ("I want__, I want___")

Activity: Finding How You Act When Angry: Remind the children that it's all right to feel anger if you express it in ways that do not hurt others or themselves. Children can learn that there are different things that they can do when they feel hurt and angry. Get them to identify what type of anger response they have. Do they pout and withdraw into hurt, explode into tantrums or displace their anger on something else? Have them decide how they like the way the form that they express their anger. The key point to get across is that they must not hurt others or themselves no matter how they feel.

EFT Tapping Phrases

   Even though I'm mad because I got a spanking, I'm still a pretty good kid.
   Even though I'm furious because my sister tattled on me, I let my anger go.
   Even though I'm mad because my brother broke my toy, I forgive myself.
   Even though I got angry when I saw a boy kick a dog, I used my anger and told him to stop.
   Even though I'm hurt and disappointed because my friend lied to me, I deal with it.
   Even though I felt ashamed when the boys teased me, I tap those feelings away.
   Even though I blew up when mom scolded me for doing something wrong, I can learn to take criticism.
   Even though I got mad when Dad didn't give me what I wanted," I tap my anger out.
   Even though I threw a fit when Mom said "No" I know I don't always get what I want.

Different Ways of Doing Aggression

<u>Goal</u>:   To understand that girls and boys do anger and aggression differently.

<u>Activity</u>:   <u>Super Hero Bear Dialogue</u>: Write the words *"aggression," "joust,"* and *"pecking order"* on the board and ask the children if they know what the words mean. Whether we like it or not, there is a pecking order to most friendships. Chickens strike and peck at each others with pounding movements to create their position in a group. People have their own pecking order as they try to get and maintain their position of power in the group.

Anger and aggressive behavior is used to joust for power just like the knights of old used to joust and knock each other off their horse with a lance to show who was stronger.

Aggression uses an attack of force to show who is in control. Aggression is behavior that uses verbal or physical force to hurt others or get them to go along with you. It is behavior that hurts others to get what you want. Some people use aggression to feel good temporarily, but feeling good when you hurt someone does not last and harms both the giver and receiver.

All groups of people have levels where people fit in. Some people are the leaders and others are the followers. Most people have some aggression in them. There are different forms of aggression that are physical or verbal. Boys and girls use different kinds of aggressive behavior to show who the leader is and who is willing to back down. You can learn how to be powerful without putting others down.

<u>Discussion Question</u>: Who is more likely to show the following types of behavior—boys or girls or both boys and girls?

> Physical aggression: Hitting, pushing, shoving, threatening, fighting and acting tough.
> Verbal aggression: Gossiping, backstabbing, mean remarks, ignoring what was said and refusing to be friends.
> Discounting, using put downs and sarcasm.
> Commanding, boasting and using anger to show being in charge.
> Asserting power by challenging each others and show off their skills and knowledge.
> Smiling, complimenting, sharing secrets and talking about feelings.

<u>EFT Taping Phrases</u>:
> Even though I have been rude to my friends to get my way, I choose to change.
> Even though I am aggressive sometimes to show I'm in charge, I learn to be friendlier.
> Even though I act in hateful ways at times, I learn to be nicer.
> Even though I spread a mean rumor about someone, I choose to stop using ugly words

<u>Tips for parents and teachers</u>: Most boys form friends through shared activities. Boys talk about things such as activities, sports and technology. Friendships are formed around the favored games such as soccer, skateboarding or computer games. To be valued by the group, it helps if the boy has skills and is competitive in order to win the game. They become a valued member of the group through their abilities and talents and earn respect and status from other boys. Girls value intimate friendships. They form groups to get close to each other and communicate by agreeing with the speaker. They use behaviors that reinforce social bonding. Some boys and girls with higher-level skills have the ability to use both forms of communication.

For more information about sex differences in friendships and brain structure and chemistry read *You Just Don't Understand: Women and Men in Communication* by Deborah Tannen and *The Essential Difference: The Truth about the Male and Female Brain* by Simon Baron-Cohen.

Weighed Down with Anger!

Objective: To release anger by talking about it before it builds up into a grudge.

Materials: Big plastic sack filled with lots of sand.

Activity: Feeling Good About Letting Anger Go: Stored, unexpressed anger as an emotion is very heavy. A grudge is when you hold on to bad feelings. Discuss how holding on to anger feels like a heavy weight on your shoulders. Holding on to bad feelings is like carrying ten pounds of sand around. Have the child get in touch with a time where he wants to hold on to his anger. Teach the child to associate this anger with being held back and weighed down.

Ask each child to describe a situation where he felt angry and heavy and held a grudge. Have him lift the sack of sand and put it is his lap or across his shoulders. Tell him he can put the sack of anger down when he uses the "I formula" and is ready to let go of his bad feelings. Remind him that feelings are just feelings and feelings are meant to be felt and released with EFT.

Some open-ended questions to ask the children to generate discussion include:

> How do you feel when you hold on to your anger? HEAVY!
> Why do we stay angry with people?
> Where do you carry your anger in your body?
> What do your hands want to do when you are angry?
> How does your stomach feel when you are angry?
> What is a grudge? Tell us about a grudge you might have?
> Sometimes we feel hurt and angry at the same time. Who can tell us about this?

What are some ways that you let go of anger? (Breathing, laughing, symbolically punching a pillow, talk it down yourself, talking to others etc.) When are some times that you should walk away and not express your feelings? (Most children can discriminate the situations when it would be dangerous to tell the other person of their anger.)

Model how speaking about the angry feelings helps you feel better. Emphasize how good it feels to let go of anger through talking about it. Stress how feelings are like the weather--always changing. Feelings come and go quickly. Hurtful feelings stick around if you hold on to them.

Build a strong association between speaking feelings and getting relief of uncomfortable feelings with this short poem. Have the children memorize the poem by repeating it several times together.

> Feelings come and feelings go.
> Some are fast and some are slow!
> When I am down and feel so low
> I talk about them and there they go!

EFT Tapping Phrases
> Even though I hold on to my mads, I'm still a likable kid.
> Event though I hide my anger away inside, I choose to let it out.
> Even though I hold on to grudges, I love and forgive myself.
> Even though I hide my hurt under anger, I breathe and let it go.
> Even though I want to hold on to my anger about _____, I'm okay just as I am.

Feelings are Powerful: Learning About Emotional Intelligence

Goals: To understand that all feelings are normal and sometimes anger can be useful.
                  To learn about Emotional Intelligence.

Activity: Guess which Feelings are Normal: Put the word "normal" on the board and define the word as many people having the same experience. Ask the children to list emotions and guess which feelings are normal. As they guess, say, "That emotion is normal. Many people have that very same feeling. Feelings have a purpose. They help us learn to trust our senses of sight, smell, taste, touch and hearing. They help us find out who we are and figure out how to act."

Activity: Anger is a Normal Emotion that can Help You: Teach the concept of anger as a neutral emotion, saying, "Anger is neither good nor bad. It is just a complex emotion that people do not know how to use correctly. Most people either deny anger and hide it deep inside or blow it out on others with a temper tantrum. You are learning how to use anger in ways that are safe and appropriate. There are times that you can use anger appropriately to be powerful. Make the word" Mad" powerful, change it to MAD—Make A Difference!"

Discussion Questions:
        When did you use anger to get an issue out in the open instead of hiding it?
        When did you use anger to clear the air instead of holding onto resentfulness?
        When did you use anger to point out a problem that needs correction?
        When did you use anger to leave a situation where you felt uncomfortable?
        When did you use anger to give yourself energy and momentum to deal with a problem?
        When did you use anger to tell someone to back off and stop doing something inappropriate?

Activity: Super Hero Bear Dialogue: "The most powerful people are those who know themselves and are in charge of their emotions. You give your power away when you respond in anger to people who tease you. Practice centering yourself and seeing those people who bother you as little gnats that try to fly in your face. Breathe deeply, center yourself and walk away. No trying to ignore them—that hasn't worked so far. Do something positive. Breathe and tell yourself you can handle whatever is thrown at you. Remind yourself that you are a cool dude who can handle upsets in life. You can take your power back by staying calm when others are acting badly with their teasing or anger."

Discuss who is more powerful:
        The person who teases to feel good or the person who says "I feel angry when you do that."
        The bully or the person who stands up to a bully or leaves the situation.
        The screaming adult or the child who watches him and breathes deeply to stay calm.
        The person who hides their anger or the one who gets it out in safe ways.

Super Hero Bear Dialogue: You can be smart in many ways—smart in reading, math or making things with your hands. Emotional Intelligence is using your emotions to become a strong person who is smart about using feelings correctly. You can use Emotional Intelligence to help you make and keep friends and have a happy life. Learning about yourself and your emotions especially the tricky ones is the best gift that you can give yourself so that you can be happy!

EFT Tapping Phrases
        Even though I give my power away by losing my temper, I choose to be strong.
        Even though I am mean to my sister, I know I can become a nicer person.
        Even though I hurt someone I cared about, I choose to stop giving away my power.
        Even though I have misused my power, I know real power is being true to myself.

Tips for parents and teachers: A recent survey of police officers showed that aggression is increasing in elementary schools and many schools do not have or do not use the resources that are available for dealing with violence and bullying. According to the survey, children are acting more aggressively at a younger age than ever before. Prevention is the key here to helping children. Teaching children to express their anger in safe ways can help break into this cycle of aggression.

I MAKE GOOD CHOICES WHEN THREATENED

I breathe to send
   oxygen to my body!

I figure out what
   is going on.

I use my firm words
   to say how I feel.

I tell the person to stop.
I leave if I am not safe.

I FEEL GOOD ABOUT TAKING CARE OF MYSELF!

How Do You See Your Anger?

Goals: To change negative images of self into positive ones.
            To learn and use self-soothing to deal with stress, threat and anger.

Activity: Make a Picture of Your Anger: Have the children draw a line down the middle of a piece of paper. On the left side, ask them to draw a picture of what their anger looks like:

I'm hot as a firecracker
I'm an emotional Yo-yo.
I'm a time bomb ready to explode
I'm a tight coil ready to spring
I have a short fuse
I'm a volcano ready to go off
There's a ball of fire within me

I'm a prisoner of my stuffed anger
I'm a pressure cooker ready to blow
There are red flames consuming me
I have a fiery temper
I'm on an emotional roller coaster
I'm stuck—my anger is engraved in stone
I'm the king/queen of denial

Have them draw a picture of Super Hero Bear on the other side of the paper giving you advice on changing the anger to something healthy. Remind the children to add some Helper Words. Have them put some good self-esteem statements in such as, "I will get through this! I'm in charge here. My out-of-control anger is not in charge."

Activity: What Do You Do when You are Upset? Ask the boys and girls to imagine that they have had a very, very bad day and feel stressed out. Ask them what they do to calm themselves down and list their answers on the board.

Write these two lists on the board with the titles "What Works for You" and "What Doesn't Work." Tally the children's responses to show things they do that makes them feel better and things that make them feel worse.

Successful Ways to Cope with Stress, Threat and Anger

Deep breathing
Praying
Talking to friends
Exercising
Listening to music
Problem solving
Distract with fun events/Hobbies

Take a walk or get out in nature
Confront self-negative verbal statements
Write about your anger
Confront others when appropriate
Find humor in situation
Take constructive action with your anger
Find a quiet place to go to in your mind

Poor Ways of Coping with Stress, Threat and Anger

Watching excessive violent TV
Not confronting the person directly
Allowing irritability to build-up and blow
Withdrawing into silent treatment
Exploding anger on others/or things

Denying problems
Personalize and hang on to anger
Stuffing feelings
Dwelling on intrusive negative thoughts
Eating to calm yourself down

Activity: Drawing Pictures in your Mind to Calm Down: Have the children close their eyes and imagine themselves upset. Then take them through several ideas from the list of positive ways of dealing with stress. Give a few ideas on each one and invite them to draw pictures in their mind of themselves becoming quieter and calmer inside. Talk to them about using the wonderful creative imagination to release stress and anger. Have them draw a picture of their Quiet Place that they can go to in their mind when they are stressed.

Tips for parents and teachers: My book, *How to Let Go of Your Mad Baggage,* gives other ideas on understanding and using anger appropriately. Here is a quote from the book: "Life is full of multidimensional possibilities. Once you get a handle on your mads, your life becomes easier and easier. Remember, you don't have to keep on doing the same-o, same-o. Choices. Life is about choices. One great thing about being a Human Being is that you do get choices. We can use our choices about our mads to become gentle, loving people. What better option do you have to do with your lifetime? Choose wisely."

Handling Discounts

Objectives: To speak feelings when threatened.
                  To listen to others when they are upset.
                  To learn to cope with a person who does not want to listen to feelings.

Activity: Handling Discount Statements: Discount statements are things that another person says to put you down when you are trying to express feelings. Discuss how some people discount by ignoring or belittling what the person speaking their feelings has said.

"Stores discount items by marking the price down. With people, discounting means to make them less than they are by not listening to them and putting them down with words. We discount someone by making them of less value when we do not listen to their words. Ways of discounting include ignoring, blaming back, getting angry and saying "I don't care how you feel.""

Have the children list some discounting statements that have been used on them when they were trying to express their upset feelings. Practice breathing for peace here. Then have the child give the other person a phrase that shows that he has been heard.

Ask the children to discriminate between people who can and those who cannot listen when others express anger. Ask them why some people have difficulty in this area. Some people are not even aware that they give children the brush off. Some adults are not comfortable in addressing feelings and are threatened when children speak their mind. Others cannot handle any type of confrontation because they have not learned the skill of listening to sensitive subjects such as anger and sadness.

Help the children to see that some people WILL NOT be able to listen to feeling statements and that is just how it is. Their job is to find someone who can hear them and support them.

Teach a response to being discounted such as "I feel really upset when you don't listen to what I have to say. Will you hear my words?" or "Don't discount what I'm saying. Please listen to me." Hearing about feelings is threatening for some people.

Phrases to Show the Person That He Has Been Heard.
    Thank you for sharing that.
    I hear what you are saying.
    When you say that to me, I feel _____. We both have a right to our feelings.
    You must have felt really _____. I hear you!

Helper Words for Children
    If he can't hear what I have to say, I'll find someone who can.
    My feelings are important. I matter to me.
    It is always okay for me to say how I feel. I carefully choose people who can listen to me.

EFT Tapping Phrases
    Even though I feel bad when someone says something mean to me, I speak up firmly.
    Even though I'm embarrassed when I'm teased, I breathe and speak my words.
    Even though I have trouble saying what I feel, I forgive myself.
    Even though speaking out is hard for me, I take a big breath and say what I need to say.

I Won't Let You Push my Buttons!

Objectives: To discover your trigger words and buttons.

                      To keep cool when others are trying to push your buttons.

Materials: Paper Plates and crayons.

Activity: Finding Your Trigger Words and Buttons: Ask the children to identify what "pushes their buttons" or trigger words. Have the children give examples of the different buttons. There are different kinds of buttons--anger, hurt and embarrassment. Buttons trigger the child to feeling a drop in self-esteem.

Not getting their way.	Not getting what they want.
Their body being hurt.	Their personal space invaded.
Being called names or teased.	Being criticized or scolded.
Their feelings discounted.	Promises broken by others.
Something being taken away from them.	Sarcastic remarks.

Challenge the children to find words and behaviors of other people that set off their anger. Ask each child to look under the anger button to see if there is hurt and shame hiding underneath. Ask the children to determine which trigger words are common to many individuals and which ones are unique to individuals. Have each child identify his own trigger words.

Ask for a volunteer to state his trigger words and get permission from him for doing this exercise. Say the trigger word to the child. Pretend to poke him in the ribs to "push his button". Remind him that he has a choice to get upset or not. Ask him to take a deep breath to keep himself from getting hurt by the trigger word. Ask him to keep a straight face and say, "I won't let you push my buttons" instead of trying to ignore the insult. This gives the child something positive to do. Ignoring hurtful remarks is hard for most children.

Role-play each situation having the child practice staying calm or laughing at a word or behavior that typically sets him off. Demonstrate to the children how they can laugh off formerly upsetting events. Laughter breaks into the power of the trigger words. Emphasize the power of being in control over their words and emotions. If a child is overly reactive to another child tell him, "Sounds like he's got your number. Maybe you need to get a unlisted number. Change your number so he can't get to you!"

Activity: Drawing the Secret Buttons: Children can learn to unhook their trigger points, and their anger, hurt and shame buttons and red-flag words. Use the paper plates to make their "buttons" by having them draw two circle in the center to designate buttonholes. Have the children draw a picture of a person using the words that upset them on the plate while they stay strong and refuse to become triggered.

Helper Words for Children

    I won't let people know my buttons. Shhh! I'll keep anger buttons a secret.

    Letting someone know my buttons and reacting to their actions gives away my power.

    If someone calls my number to make me mad, I change my number! I keep my new number unlisted!

    I don't have to get mad or hurt when someone tries to tease me.

    I breathe to let the teasing words roll off my back.

    I can keep my cool. I do cool stuff! I say, "Oh, he is just trying to push my buttons!"

    If he tries to tease me, I'll say, "My buttons are not for pushing."

EFT Tapping Phrases

    Even though I get mad when people tease me, I'm still a great kid.

    Even if I lose my cool when my buttons are pushed, I accept myself.

    Even though I react badly when called names, I forgive myself.

I Can Listen to Your Unhappy Feelings

Objective: To listen to negative feelings.

Activity: Role Playing Listening to Angry Feelings: Children enjoy role playing conflict situations as it gives them an opportunity to act out their grievances while learning a new skill. Set up imaginary situations while the children are learning the skill of listening to angry feelings of others. Adding some silly phrases like "You have a green bean on your nose." or "Yesterday you were a kangaroo." decreases the tension in this activity.

Role Playing Examples:
>   One child runs into another on the playground.
>   One child teases another child and calls him "stupid."
>   One child grabs another child's lunch box and taunts him to try to get it back.
>   The big brother won't let the younger child have a turn choosing a television show.

Model breathing deeply while listening when someone describes his feelings to you. Ask for two volunteers to play the two roles. Praise the child who shares and the other who listens. When they are finished with the role-playing, ask each child how he feels. Remind them that sharing feelings is to help them feel better and not to try to change the other person.

Activity: Sharing Real-Life Feelings: Choose an emotionally strong, resilient child who could hear some negative feelings to be the listener. Remind him to take a deep breath and feel good about himself. Exaggerate this breath at first to bring humor into the situation. The next step is to ask for a volunteer to air some upsetting feelings. Coach him on what he might say.

Stand behind the receiver to support him by stage whispering in his ear that he can listen and handle the situation. Remind him to breathe away any feelings of threat or fear that may come up. Have the listener say, "Thanks for sharing."

At the end of the role-playing, ask each child how he feels now. Praise both children for having the courage to deal with a situation by expressing feelings. Play up the fact that the initial feelings have shifted from anger and fear to pride and accomplishment. Encourage the group to clap for the child who has taken a risk in sharing her feelings and for the one who was able to hear those feelings.

Cues
>   If you don't like what ____ is doing, tell him. You need to use your feeling words and a firm voice.
>   Can you listen to what she has to say? You don't need to be scared to listen to feelings.
>   Ask him if he will hear what you have to say. Ask him if he will hear your words.
>   I'm glad you could hear her words without your getting angry in return. Great listening!
>   Pat yourself on the back for standing there and listening to why she was upset.

Helper Words for Children
>   I can listen to people who share hurt or angry feelings.
>   I'll take a deep breath and listen to how upset she is.
>   Children are to be seen and heard and to be believed.
>   I am powerful when I "own" my mistakes.

EFT Tapping Phrases
>   Even though I don't want to hear what I did wrong, I deal with it.
>   Even though I hate hearing criticism, I listen and learn and then feel good about myself.
>   Even though it is scary being criticized, I can take it.
>   Even though I dislike hearing that someone is angry, I listen and learn from it.
>   Even though I made a mistake, I admit it, fix it and move on.

I CAN SAY I'M SORRY

I can listen to your upset feelings.

I'm big enough to hear what you say.

I'M A PEOPLE FRIENDLY PERSON.

Letting the Mads Out

Objective: To identify the location of anger that is held in the body.
                        To learn symbolic ways of safely releasing anger.

Materials: Play Dough and small table to work on.

Activity: <u>Where I Hide My Mads</u>: Talk to the children about the place in their bodies where they hold on to the bad feelings. Most children identify their stomachs, chests or arms and hands. For some children, it is in their head as they have angry thoughts. Ask the children to feel the anger that they carry and tell them that they can learn to let it go.

Give each child a small piece of play dough. As each child tells his story, ask the other children if they have ever had a similar situation. Express your concern and sympathy about the stories. Show the children how to bring the anger up from their stomach, through the chest, down the arms and put it into the fists. Pound the play dough to show the children how to transfer the anger out of their hands into the dough.

Say to the children, "Now if you are angry with someone, let that anger out and put it in the play dough. Pound it, that's right, pound it hard." Say out loud, 'Mad. Mad. Mad. I'm mad. I'm mad. I'm mad at you _____.' Pound, pound, pound hard and let it go! Tell yourself, "I can tell people and use my words when I am angry." Putting words to feelings in a chant like this will help children call forth hidden anger. Tell the children, "If you are mad at your mom or dad, take that mad and let it go up, up, up through your body, down your arm and into your fists. Now pound it out saying "Mad, mad, mad, I'm really mad'. Use your words. Pound that clay hard and send the mad stuff right out your fingers. Remember we can't hurt people but we can put the mads in a safe place. If you are mad at your brother tell him, "I'm mad at you." Tell your sister, "I'm mad at you." Tell yourself, "I can let go of my anger. I can say my anger and let it go. I can feel good about telling my mads and letting them go." At the end of this activity, sigh with relief and remind them that anger is a temporary feeling that can be released.

Go through several other situations of children's frustrations such as someone grabbing their toy or teasing them. Ask the children, "Do we hit people? No, but we can put our mads in this clay. You can leave your anger here in this clay." Assure the children that everyone gets mad now and then, but it can be hurtful to the body to hold on to anger and that it is okay to get mad if you handle it in a way that does not injure others.

Ask what other things they could pound on (pillows, a mattress, hammering on a throw a way aluminum pie plate or piece of Styrofoam to release their mads. Continue to remind the children that while it is never allowable to hurt people, the play dough can absorb all the anger that they can give it. They can choose to let their mads out by punching something that is safe

<u>Cues</u>
    You can put your mads somewhere safe instead of acting them out.
    You need to go take care of your bad feelings. Figure out how to let them go.
    I know you can work out this anger. What are some things you could do with it?

<u>Helper Words for Children</u>
    I deal with my mads when they come up. I find a safe place to store my mads.
    I can use laughter and movement to let my anger go.
    I watch my anger drain out of my brain and into something safe.

<u>Tips for parents and teachers</u>: The kids who are not angry with their parents will not put much energy in this activity but will find it fun. Angry children will typically react with much energy. The children who express the most anger will need a "talking debriefing" and some EFT tapping after this activity to process their remaining anger.

Even if I Say My Mads, I Still Have to Mind My Parents

Objective: To learn symbolic ways of safely releasing anger.

Materials: Play Dough and small table to work on and the page, *I Let Go of My Mads*.

Activity: <u>I Know I have to Mind My Parents</u>: Sometimes children express anger at small things that their parents require of them. Some children believe that they do not have to mind adults if they use their "I feel _____ when you _____" statements. Some children express anger inappropriately about having to pick up their toys, having to go to bed, or their parent not buying them a toy at the store. Remind them that this is a situation where they are making themselves miserable by getting angry. Remind them that they always have choices. Even if they say the "I feel _____ when, you _____." They still have to obey the rules.

Using the Play Dough, use the heel of your hand to symbolically release the negative feelings. Remind the children that they can choose to express their anger in a safe place by using their words and then letting it go. Show the children how to send the anger to the fingers and pinch the play dough. Put the anger in the play dough by pinching it all over while the group chants,

> I feel good about putting my mads in a safe place.
> Mads come, mads go. I can let my anger go!
> I get what I get and I don't have a fit.
> I separate the Big Deals from the Little Deals. Having to do chores is a Little Deal.
> I become part of the solution instead of part of the problem.
> Chores just have to be done. I finish quickly, and then off to fun.

Activity: <u>Take down the volcano</u>: Another variation is to use the Play Dough to make a volcano (which symbolizes their mads building up) and the smashing of it. Talk to the children about how anger can be like a exploding volcano. If they allow their mads to build up, they will explode! Ask them to remove tiny pinches of the clay dough volcano until it is completely gone.

By this time you will notice some of the children becoming weary of this activity and starting to make creative forms out of the play dough. Ask them to check the place where they store their bad feelings to see if any are left. You may notice that some of the children will become silly or more relaxed after this activity.

Ask the children to check again and put any last piece of anger into their play dough. Collect the play dough and assure the children that their stored-away anger will be safe up on the shelf. Show them how to dust off their hands by slapping them together to indicate that they are finished with their anger for now. Have them shake their arms and flick out their wrists and fingers to signify throwing off any anger. Then have them pat themselves on the back for doing a good job of getting their mads out!

<u>Helper Words for Children</u>
> I can feel good about letting go of my anger.
> Mads come, mads go. I can let my anger GO!
> Shake it out. Shake out my anger. I can let that anger go.

<u>EFT Tapping Phrases</u>
> Even though I say my feelings, I still have to mind my parents.
> Even though I didn't get what I wanted, I just deal with it.
> Even though I get mad when I have to do chores, I choose to be calm and confident.
> Even though I don't want to pick up my room, I'm still an awesome kid.
> Even though I don't want to go to bed, I deal with it.

Parents Fight. That is a Grownup Problem

Objectives: To learn techniques of self-soothing.
                      To learn to take care of self during parental arguments.

Materials: The *How I Take Care of Myself When Grown-ups Fight* page.

Activity: I Find Ways To Take Care of Myself: Dealing with parents' arguments is one of the most stressful things for children. Children need to learn to leave when their parents fight and find things to do that help them feel better about themselves. Talk to the children about how all parents argue and fight and then make up. Teach this chant, having the children repeat the lines in unison.

> Grown-ups fight.
> Grown-ups make up.
> It is a grown-up problem.
> It is not my problem.
> I'll go take care of myself.

Discuss healthy and unhealthy ways children take care of themselves when parents are fighting. Unsuccessful tactics during parental conflict include standing and watching the fight or trying to get in the middle of the fight and defend one of the parents. These choices generally make the child feel more helpless as he does not have enough power to break into the negative energy that is present during times of conflict. Hand out the worksheet How I Take Care of Myself When Grown-ups Fight and discuss ways children act when their parents fight.

Give the children permission to leave the angry scene and go to their room or outside to play where they don't have to hear the angry words. Discuss various options that they can choose to take during family conflict. A better way for the child to take care of himself is to remove himself from the stressful situation and do something to distract his mind away from the conflict. Discuss several things children can do during parental conflict. Safe activities include going to their room and shutting the door, turning on music or television, using headphones to block out sound, stroking and holding a pet, going outside or to the neighbors or finding another safe place to be (closet, under the covers, etc.) Explain to the children that if people are being physically hurt, they can call 911 or go to the neighbors to ask for help. Role play, dealing with adult conflict, with children playing the roles of the fighting parents. Have one child take the role of making a good choice to take care of himself.

Cues
    You are just a little kid. You don't need to be involved in grown-ups fights.
    You can choose to leave when people are upset with each other.
    When you feel bad inside, find things to do that make you feel good.

EFT Tapping Phrases
    Even though I get worried when my parents fight, I take care of myself.
    Even though it is scary when my parents argue, I'm not the cause of their problems.
    Even though I get upset and afraid when grownups yell, I let them handle their problem.
    Even though I get mad when my mom and dad fight, I tap to let the bad feelings go.
    Even though I'm afraid my folks will get a divorce when they fight, it's just a fight.

Tips for parents and teachers: Parental fighting is one of the greatest causes of anxiety and trauma in children. The role of choice and the permission to act in one's best behalf is important in good self-esteem. Giving the child the choice to break out of his habitual response to parental conflict will help him deal with the negative affect that is being expressed. Permission to take care of oneself instead of staying and being part of the negative energy gives the worried child relief. Copy the following worksheet to send home with a note saying that this may not be a problem in all families but that children still need this skill of taking care of themselves during conflict over which they have no control.

HOW CAN I TAKE CARE OF MYSELF WHEN GROWNUPS FIGHT?

Try to get in the fight to protect one of the people.

Act silly and distract them.

Feel bad inside. Feel responsible for one of the people.

Act tough and pretend it doesn't bother me.

Go away, take care of myself and remember that it is a grownup problem.

Here is what I can do. I talk to my parents to get their ideas.
I tell my parents how I feel when grownups are angry.

Signed: _____ Date: _____

(Parent/Guardian) Signed: _____ Date: _____

46

Taking Good Care of Myself When I'm Upset

Objective: To learn techniques of self-soothing when stressed and upset.

Activity: I Can Make My Own Body Feel Good!: Children who are upset and hurt need to learn ways to take care of themselves when they have uncomfortable feelings. Talk to the children about things that they did when they were little to feel safe such as holding on to their blanket or sucking a pacifier or their thumb. Ask them what they do when they are feeling insecure to take care of themselves. Ideas include holding a favorite stuffed animal or gaining comfort from a pet, rocking, taking a warm bath or listening to music. Talking to a friend is another positive way to deal with stress.

Activity: Rubbing Your Skin to Feel Good: Talk to the children about how the skin is the largest organ of the body. The skin is the receiver of touch, which can be soothing. Discuss how scratching, touching and massage release the good chemicals in the brain to help people feel better. These positive brain chemicals are called endorphins and can be activated by stimulating the scalp and skin. Show them how briskly rubbing their arms is invigorating.

Patting their body briskly is another form of self-massage, which helps bring about relaxation. Have the children start at the back of the head and pat across the scalp and down their face and the front of their body. Demonstrate how to pat up and down the fronts and backs of the legs and arms and as much of their back they can reach.

Show the children how to stimulate a few of the trigger points on the body to release endorphins. Pinching the web between the thumb and first finger or pressing firmly on the temples can sometimes release stress and pain.

Children often release stress by nail biting, hair twirling, restlessness and hyperactivity. Tell the children that there are different activities to release such as rolling a marble in the hands, rubbing a smooth worry stone or tucking the thumb into the other fingers while breathing deeply. And of course, tapping.

Activity: I Can Give Myself a Big Bear Hug: Show the children how to hug themselves by wrapping their arms around their bodies in a big bear hug. Super Hero Bear can demonstrate his hugging himself. End your daily activities by telling the children to pat themselves on the back for their accomplishments as an exercise in feeling good. Tell the children to say to themselves "I'll give myself a big pat on the back for what I learned."

Cues
      Take care of your bad feelings and you will take care of yourself.
      Always make a good choice and be gentle and loving with yourself.
      Love your body. Be gentle and loving with your body.
      Ask for permission before you touch someone else's body.
      You are a special person and deserve good things.

Helper Words for Children
      It is okay for me to show how I feel.
      I can soothe myself when I am upset.
      Hurting inside is a signal to find a friend to talk to.
      If I'm having a hard day, I'll give myself a hug and tell myself to deal with it.
      I'll do loving things to take care of myself.
      I deserve to feel good about myself.

Tips for parents and teachers: Learning to use self-soothing techniques to reduce anxiety can decrease the use of alcohol, drugs and increased food intake in later life. Learning positive means of reducing anxiety and feeling good when stressed helps people avoid addictive behavior.

I Learn Anger Management Skills

I Channel Anger Into Constructive Action

☐ I feel and name my emotions as they come up. I tell myself they are just feelings to be felt.

☐ I use the "I formula" when I am angry or upset to state my feelings.

☐ I confront others who discount my feelings and do not want to listen.

☐ I express anger in safe and productive ways to increase my self-esteem.

☐ I use my anger constructively. I change *MAD* to mean "Make A Difference" with my anger.

☐ I choose to not speak my feelings when it's not safe to do so.

☐ I put my anger into safe objects such as pounding a pillow when it's not safe to express it directly.

☐ I break into my self-angering thoughts and cool myself down with Helper Words.

I Learn Assertive Ways of Dealing with Threat

☐ I stand up and speak assertively when threatened.

☐ I say "No" when others ask me to do something wrong. I state my boundaries.

☐ I leave the situation when the other person does not respect my boundaries.

☐ I shield myself against name-calling and ridicule. I see the ugly words as negative energy.

☐ I take care of myself when others fight.   I remember that it's not my problem. It's their problem.

☐ I stop numbing out and use deep breathing to stay present to deal with the problem.

I Learn to Contain Excessive Anger

☐ I don't sweat the small stuff. I make a distinction between big deals and little deals.

☐ I know that I don't always get what I want. I use Helper Words to keep me from becoming angry.

☐ I stop the irrational thoughts that fuel my anger and break into them with Helper Words.

☐ I stop my hot thoughts and use cool down thoughts when I notice that I am angry.

☐ I analyze and correct my mistakes instead of beating myself up.

☐ I keep my cool when others tease me and try to push my buttons.

☐ I take a Time Out when overheated during an argument to cool myself down.

☐ I stop using sarcasm and put downs when I am angry at someone.

☐ I use The Emotional Freedom Technique to release my anger.

I Learn to Feel Empathy and Respect Others

☐ I stop and think before teasing or bullying others and consider how my actions might hurt their feelings.

☐ I stop blaming others when I am angry or stressed out. I consider my own part in the situation.

☐ I take responsibility for my own actions and wrong doings.

☐ I listen to others when they are upset and honor their feelings even if I disagree with them.

☐ I learn to walk in the other person's shoes and see things from their perspective.

☐ I observe the effect of my behavior upon others and say "I am sorry."

☐ I treat my friends, family and strangers with respect and caring.

I Observe Rather than Over React to Threatening Events

☐ I watch my body reactions and emotions during threat and slow down my anger response.

☐ I find and express the hurt, sadness and confusion that hide under my anger.

☐ I stop beating myself up when things go wrong. I use Helper Words to get me through bad times.

☐ I make self-empowering statements and tell myself that I can deal with the situation.

☐ I increase my self-esteem by changing inappropriate anger responses to ones that are more effective.

☐ I use techniques of self-soothing when I am upset.

Tips for parents and teachers: Some of these skills are not taught in this book; they are included in the lesson plans in I Stop My Bully Behavior and The Anger Works Kit (lesson plans for teaching children who have been abused) and are available at the www.AngriesOut.com web site.

Feel Your Feelings and Think Your Thoughts

Objective: To distinguish between thoughts and feelings.

Materials: Drawing page, *I Draw My Feelings.*

Activity: <u>Group Discussion and Drawing</u>: A thought is something you think--"I feel like getting out of here." is a thought with an action to it. Feelings are grounded in the body. Feelings can best be taught by using the feeling words "sad, mad, bad, glad, scad" and then branching off to access other feelings such as disappointment, frustration, etc.

Numbing is an Unfeeling which pushes other feelings way deep down inside. You get numb sometimes when you are so scared that you just stop feeling. Numbness can be explored, brought up and transformed into the scary feelings, which then can be released with EFT. Ask the children to distinguish between these thoughts (an action) or feelings (emotions. Ask them to distinguish between something they want to do or whether they actually feel sad, mad, bad, glad, scad or another feeling.

I'm upset.	I feel angry when you glare at me.
I feel like sitting down.	I was unhappy when he told me the news.
I feel like having a cool drink.	I feel like going home.

Cues
Let your true feelings out. Check under the numbness to see what else is there.
It's a good idea to talk about things that are bothering you.
If you are feeling sad or mad inside, let it show. Make your face and feelings match.
Share your sad feelings and then you can let them go.
Take care of yourself and your feelings. Do things that make you happy with yourself.

Helper Words for Children
I feel sad and hurt. I'll find someone to share these feelings with.
I can take care of myself by talking about my hurt feelings.
It's okay for me to ask for help when I am upset.
I'll find someone safe to talk to about my feelings.
Feelings come and feelings go. I can let my feelings go!

EFT Tapping Phrases
Even though it is hard to say my feelings, I'm learning how to be healthy with them.
Even though I'd rather ignore my bad feelings, I choose to get them out.
Even though I want to stuff my feelings, I love and forgive myself.
Even though it is easier for me to hide my feelings, I know I need to get them out safely.
Even though I feel numb when scared, I tap to find my real feelings and then tap them away.

<u>Tips for parents and teachers</u>: Notice the expression on their faces as the children talk. Some children show a lot of emotion as they relate their experiences. Others report with a blank facial expression in an apparently non-emotional manner. If the child has a smile on his face as he talks about something painful, he may be embarrassed or making up a story. He may have learned to repress his true feelings. He may have been taught that it is not appropriate to talk about sensitive subjects. Matching the inner feelings with the same facial expression helps the child release the negative feelings. Feelings shift easier when there is consistency in body posture, feelings inside, voice tone, content of what is being expressed and facial expression. Remind the children to let their feelings, body, face and talk all match. Or to "Let your outsides match your insides!" Remind them that it feels bad to be hurting inside and not be able to talk about it.

The Bad Feelings Part

Objective: To help understand negative emotions.
                    To help deal with shame.

Materials: The Bad Feelings Part

Activity: I'm Too Embarrassed to Tell You Who I Am: Bring out the Bad Feelings Part to talk to the children. Push his head down on his chest and have him talk in an embarrassed, mumbling manner. Make him reluctant to talk at first and encourage the children to ask questions to draw him out. Let the Bad Feeling Part talk to the children saying:

"Well, I don't want to talk. I don't want to tell you who I am. No, don't try to get me to talk. I just want to hide-away. Yes, yes, I am a part of you. I'm a part of everybody, but I don't like to talk about it. Just leave me alone. Don't make me tell my secrets of how bad I feel inside. I hide away inside everybody. Generally down in their tummy. I have to hide because I don't want anyone to know I'm here. If they knew I was here, they might laugh at me. So I keep myself in hiding. You won't laugh at me will you? Oh good. If you laughed, I'd run and hide, and you would never get to know me.

"Have you guessed who I am by now? Do you know which part of you I represent? It's so hard for me to be talking to you. How do I know you won't tease me or scold me? That is how I get started--someone teases a child and the bad feelings get born. I get born when someone hurts a child. Or makes a child feel bad by calling them names like stupid or dummy or even worse.

"Sometimes I get born when a young person feels that they are different. Like they look different or have different clothes. Or that they can't do things that other children their own age can. Or when they have done something that was wrong. Or made a mistake. Then the person starts to feel bad inside. Whoops! I almost told you. I almost told you my name. I'd better get back in hiding. I don't want you to know who I am." (Ask the children to reassure The Bad Feelings Part that it is safe. Ask them to guess his name. Have them ask him to tell more of his story.)

"Well, now you know. Yes, I'm the Bad Feeling Part. It's so hard for me to talk. It hurts to talk about the bad feelings, like feeling ashamed and embarrassed. It's hard to talk about these things. I've hidden away for so long. I've almost lost my voice. I've forgotten how to talk. Do you really want to know about me? You can help me talk about my bad feelings if you share your bad feelings with me.

Some people hurt so bad inside that they cannot even know about their bad feelings. They think they don't have any yucky feelings inside. Their bad feelings are hidden so deep they don't know about them. Yes, you might have some of me in you. Everyone has bad feelings about something. Boys, girls, and grownups-all sorts of people can have bad feelings. People who have been teased or hurt a lot have more bad feelings inside them. I'm here to help you learn to talk about your bad feelings and get them out!"

Discussion Questions
What bad feelings do you have in you? Who can tell us about feelings that are yucky? Who can tell us about feeling embarrassed? Who has feelings of being ashamed inside? How do you feel after sharing your yucky feelings?

EFT Tapping Phrases
    Even though I did something bad, I learn from it and let it go.
    Even though I feel bad after goofing up, I admit it, fix it and move on.

Tips for parents and teachers: Shame is a powerful emotion that contributes to children's denial, secrecy and misbehavior. Your compassion and understanding about the bad feelings that children have will help them talk about them and release them.

The Bad Feeling Part Causes Me to Act Out

Objective: To learn that trouble sometimes accompanies the bad feelings.
                          To learn that discussing uncomfortable feelings brings relief.

Materials: Bad Feeling Part, Mad Part and Trouble Part

Activity: I Avoid the Bad Feelings by Disguising Myself and Causing Trouble: Have the Bad Feeling Part talk to the children saying:

"Sometimes when I am hurting so bad inside I want to shut the bad feelings down so I take on a disguise." Do you know what a disguise is? People wear disguises to hide who they are. Have you ever worn a disguise? Some people disguise their feelings. They hide what they really feel and pretend something else. Sometimes we act one way and feel a different way inside. Like happy on the outside but sad or bad on the inside. Do you know about pretending to feel different from what is going on inside?

Sometimes I feel so bad inside and don't want others to know about it. The bad feelings are so uncomfortable. Then I start to act out. Maybe my Mad Part comes out. My Trouble Part comes out so I don't have to feel bad, embarrassed, uncomfortable or ashamed. My Trouble Part takes over. The Trouble Part is really me acting out the bad feelings. Do you know about the Trouble Part? It is that part of you that has hands and feet and a mouth that does hurtful things. Your Trouble Part acts out when you want to shut the bad feelings down inside. So you act tough. Or mean. Or do sneaky things. Or say things that are hurtful to someone else. Everybody has a Trouble Part. If you learn about it and take care of it, it won't need to act out so much."

Discussion Questions
Where do you hide bad feelings in your body?
Who can share some yucky feelings about something they did wrong?
Who feels bad inside because someone called them a bad name?
Tell us about feeling bad inside because you wanted to do something that is hard but couldn't.
Tell about a time when someone did something mean to you and then laughed.
Do your hands, feet or big mouth get you in trouble?
Does your head go down and the bad feelings come up when you get scolded?

Helper Words for Children
I can use my Helper Words to help me get my bad feelings out.
When I feel scared, I'll tell myself, "Go ahead and talk about it."
I tell myself, "I feel good about working this out."
I use my words to take my power. Helper Words make me feel powerful.
I can feel good about letting go of my yucky feelings. I'll send those bad feelings to the moon.

EFT Tapping Phrases
Even though I hide my hurt and act out in ways that hurt others I try to change.
Even though my Bad Feelings Part has been out, I'll tap on it.
Even though I feel yucky inside sometimes, I tap until I feel better.
Even though my Trouble Part acts out my bad feelings, I forgive myself.
Even though I act tough and mean to hide feeling bad inside, I learn and grow.

Tips for parents and teachers: When the Trouble, Sad and Mad Parts of the personality animals are presented in a light-hearted, matter-of-fact way, children feel safe in finding similar parts in themselves. With a caring adult who empathize with their uncomfortable feelings, the children can start to let go of negative labels and beliefs about themselves. They can substitute the concepts of the Trouble, Mad and Sad Parts instead of defining themselves generically as "bad." They can learn that they are human and have normal negative emotions that they can understand and deal with in safe ways.

I Am Many Parts—The Sad Part

Objectives: To understand and express feelings of sadness and hurt.

                         To understand that feelings are temporary and can be released when talked about.

Materials: The stuffed animals representing the Sad Part, Bad Feelings Part and Super Hero Bear.

Activity: <u>Introduce the children to the Sad Part</u>: "The Sad Part feels sad because he hurts inside. Someone or something has hurt this part. The Sad Part hunches over and feels like crying. He needs to talk to someone about his hurting feelings. Here is the Bad Feelings Part who might hang around with the Sad Part. Your sads stay around longer if you don't talk about what makes you sad. Sometimes the Sad Part hides under the Mad Part.

<u>Discussion Questions for Finding the Sad Part</u>
> What do you think made this Sad Part upset?
> Tell me what made your Sad Part come out.
> Have you had the sads and the mads at the same time?
> Tell me about a time when someone hurt your body.
> Were you ever sad seeing someone else or an animal being hurt?
> Have you ever lost anything and felt sad about it?
> Tell us about a time when someone you loved died and you were really sad.

<u>Super Hero Bear Comments to the Sad Part</u>: Have the child hold the Sad Part while you hold the Super Hero Bear. Have Super Hero Bear "talk" to the Sad Part and Bad Feelings Part using statements like these:

> Who has some sads inside them?
> I'm sorry for what has happened to you. How did you feel?
> Tell me about your hurt feelings.
> You must have felt really bad about that. Tell us about it.
> Did anyone else have an experience like that?
> What did you do when you felt bad inside?
> Is there anything else you could do rather than go away by yourself and feel bad?
> How can you take care of yourself when you feel upset?
> What are some things you can do to make yourself feel better? (Draw a picture, listen to music, pet an animal, read a book, rock, hug yourself, talk to someone who cares, etc.).
> Feelings come, feelings go. Tell us about a time your sad feelings went away.
> Was there a bit of the Mad Part that went along with your Sad Part?
> I'm glad you can talk about your sad feelings. Now you can let them go.

Give the two parts and the Super Hero Bear to each child who talks. Help the child choose Helper Words that he could have Super Hero Bear say to the Sad and Bad Feelings Parts. She may do this talking out loud or nonverbally if painfully shy. Playing both parts helps the child internalize the Super Hero Bear talk and work through some of the issue by herself.

<u>EFT Tapping Phrases:</u>
> Even though I can't stand these sad feelings, I hang out and tap them until they leave.
> Even though I hate having these sad feelings, they are a part of life and I can let them go.
> Even though I feel sad and bad inside, I can use EFT tapping and let them go.
> Even though I'm sad because someone I loved died, I know these feelings are normal.
> Even though my Sad Part has gotten big, I'm still an awesome kid.
> Even though I hide my hurt feelings under my anger, I choose to let these feelings go.

I Draw or Write to Take Care of My Bad Feelings

Objective: To learn to draw and write to release feelings.
                         To learn self-soothing activities.

Materials: Sad Part, Mad Part, Bad Feelings Part, Super Hero Bear, Crayons and paper.

Activity: Group Discussion: Talk with the children about taking good care of themselves when they feel sad. Remind them that it is so important that they do something to help get the bad feelings out to make them feel better. Have Super Hero Bear talk to the children about self-soothing activities or neat things they can do to work out the unhappy feelings.

Discussion questions for problem solving about releasing bad feelings

      Tell us about a time you used your crayons or pencil to get bad feelings out.
      Do you have a favorite blanket, stuffed toy, pet or safe place to go when you are upset?
      Have you ever used special music to change your mood?
      Other children like to move--they ride their bike, exercise, dance or rock back and forth. Have you ever used movement to work your bad feelings out?
      What are some things people do that are not helpful or even possibly harmful? (Eat, hurt someone, go off by yourself and hide your feelings)
      Who do you turn to when you have a problem? Who helps you solve your own problems?

Sometimes the child wants to hold on to the stuffed animal representing the Sad or Mad Part. He literally will not want to give the animals back to you. Acknowledge to the child that he is not quite ready to let that part go yet. Respect his need to fully express his anger or sadness nonverbally by simply holding on to the Sad, Mad or Bad Feelings Parts. Remind him that while it is all right to hold on to angry or sad feelings but at some point he might want to feel something different.

The child will let go of uncomfortable feeling when he is ready. However, if he remains in a traumatic situation at home or on the playground, he will not be able to let the bad feelings completely go until the situation changes. All the same, he will feel better for having someone to empathetically listen to his pain.

Activity: Drawing: When they feel bad, most children isolate themselves and stay stuck in feeling hurt. Talk with the children about their unhappy feelings using the Sad, Mad and Bad Feeling Parts. Have them draw a picture of unhappy things that happened to them. If they choose, you can write their story for them as they draw. Children often feel better after expressing their emotions graphically.

Children also can discharge negative emotions by writing about their feelings. Even very young children who have not mastered the skill of writing feel better when they "scribble write" about their sad story and their feelings. Sometimes covering the entire page with heavy black scribble writing will help a child release her unhappy feelings. She may or may not want to share the story that goes with the drawing.

Tips for parents and teachers: The research shows that writing about feelings 15 minutes a day helps people release unhappy experiences and strengthens their immune system! Encourage children to take a time out to take care of their feelings. You might have a "Take care of your feelings corner" in the room that has crayons and paper where children could volunteer to go draw or write when they feel upset.

I Draw My Feelings

Sad:

Mad:

Bad:

Glad:

Scad (Made up word for scared):

Other feelings:

Remember, thoughts are thoughts. Feelings are feelings.
I find my true feelings. I speak my feelings.

I Am Many Parts: The Baby Part and the Happy Part

Objectives: To discuss the need to act younger than you are.
                    To learn to do things that make you feel happy.

Materials: The Baby Part and the Happy Part

Activity: Finding My Baby Part: The Baby Part has two different parts--the need for affection and regression to an infantile state. The Positive Baby Part wants to be petted, stroked and held. It is the part that wants nurturing from others. It wants to be snuggled and loved. It wants others to make it feel better by showing affection and caring. Everyone has a Baby Part inside although some people pretend that they are tough and don't want to be loved." Ask the children how they want family members to show them love and affection.

The negative aspect of the Baby Part is not wanting to grow up. The youngest child in a family is sometimes reinforced in remaining the "baby" and resists acting in a manner appropriate for his age.

Dialogue: "Here is the Baby Part who doesn't want to act his age. He says, "I can't. Help me. Do it for me." Sometimes this part talks baby talk. Sometimes it acts much younger than its age. It feels helpless. This part comes out sometimes when a new baby of themselves is born into the family. Maybe it comes out when you are tired or sick. Does anyone have a Baby Part like this that they can talk about?"

Discussion Questions for Finding the Two Baby Parts
    Who would like to pet the Baby Part as you talk about it?
    What do you want him or her to do?
    Tell me about how you like to be held and petted.
    Talk about how good it feels to have someone tuck you in bed at night.

    Sometimes you pretend and act much younger than you are. Tell us about this.
    Have you ever wanted to go back to being a baby or a much younger child?
    Let's all talk baby talk for just one minute. Why do you think people talk baby talk?
    Which of the two baby parts do you like? Which one do you not like? Why not?
    Why do you think some children act much younger at home?

Activity: I Find My Happy Part: The Happy Part comes out when we feel good about ourselves. It is there when we are cheerful and nothing much bothers us. It sings, laughs dances and plays. Even when your Sad Part is outside, the Happy Part is always there waiting to come out. When you share your feelings, the Mad, Sad and Trouble Parts can get smaller and the Happy Part comes back.

Super Hero Bear Comments to Remembering the Happy Part
    Tell me about your Happy Part. You can hold it as you talk.
    What makes you happy? What make you feel soooooo good?
    What is the best thing that happened to you this week? In your whole life?
    What did you do to make your Happy Part come out recently?
    Tell us how you feel when the Happy Part comes out.

Tips for parents and teachers: These Parts of the Personality, represented by stuffed animals, give the children opportunities to talk directly about the hurt that they have experienced. They help children diffuse shame and other negative feelings that have built up. Hearing other children talk helps the child realize that he is not the only one who has felt this way. The children identify with the different parts and project their repressed feelings upon the stuffed animals representing the different parts. Children can learn from each other as they share their hurts in the safety of the group.

I Am Special and Loved Part

Objective: To learn to feel good about who you are.

Materials: Red heart--Special Part that knows it is loved, Super Hero Bear and the Sad Part.

Activity: I Know I Am Loved: The Special Part who knows that it is loved is a very wise part. It wants the best for you. All we want is to be loved and accepted. Sometimes when we don't get attention and affection in the way we want, we act out. Tell me about a time when you felt very good inside because you knew that you were loved. (Some children do not feel love from their parents. Sadly enough, some children may be able to respond only when you suggest a relative or pet that gave them unconditional love. Be sensitive here allowing those children who do not want to answer to remain quiet. Some may be embarrassed by the question.)

Bring out the Sad Part again. Ask the children to tell of something that happened to them that caused their heart to shut down. This experience may be of great anger or hurt so that they closed off part of themselves and stopped trusting someone. Express your sadness or whatever you feel as you hear these stories.

Hand the Super Hero Bear to the child after he describes a painful situation. Ask the child to have Super Hero Bear talk to him about what happened. The Super Hero and the Special Part can work together to give the child messages about positive self-esteem. Give the Special Part to the child when he has finished talking about a painful issue reminding him that he can feel good about himself for discussing it. Remind the children that they are special and deserve to be loved.

Activity: Free Play: Encourage the children to play with the stuffed animal and create a dialogue to express hidden themes and agendas. A few children may engage in what looks like aggressive behavior with the Super Hero Bear. This aggression may be the child's way of working through the issue. Free play with toys to work out issues is one of the main ideas behind Play Therapy.

The children seem to get some satisfaction by just flying Super Hero Bear and another part through the air while they talk to themselves. Their dialogue appears to be trying to work out some inner conflict between their anger and wanting to do better. Some children use the parts and Super Hero Bear to discover a peaceful solution to a problem on their own.

Helper Words for Children
    Super Hero Bear and I can figure it out.
    It's okay to remember that I am loved even when I'm feeling bad.
    When I share my Sad Part with someone, my Happy Part will come back.

EFT Tapping Phrases
    Even though I don't feel loved at times, I choose to be kind to myself.
    Even though I feel unloved when I'm punished, I forgive myself. I remember I am lovable.
    Even though I shut down my happiness when something bad happened, I forgive myself.
    Even though at times I feel bad about myself, I know I am a good kid overall.
    Even though I shut down my heart when something bad happened, I can open it again.
    Even though I don't feel loved when I do something bad, I forgive myself.

Tips for parents and teachers: Children who do not feel loved can become secretive and lonely or bullies. A few children may say that they do not feel loved. They may believe this either in general or at this specific time of their lives. Feeling unloved may be due to the child's acting out and feeling bad or adults in their life hurting him or neglecting him. Ask these children to find a time they did feel love from a pet, relative or a tree or inanimate object such as a teddy bear. You might try to find a Big Brother or Sister or surrogate grandparent or ask other adults to watch out for these children and give them loving attention.

More and More Parts!

Objective: To find other parts waiting to be discovered.

Materials: Collection of other stuffed animals and a sack or basket to hold them.

Activity: Finding Other Parts: Bring various types of stuffed animals to the classroom. Designate the parts who represent the skills and talents that are known or yet to be discovered. Children can be quite creative about finding parts that they need to talk about. For example:

> The Creative Part
> The Part that is Good or Not-so-Good at Sports
> The Part That Is Good At Math
> The Musical Part

Use your imagination in developing other parts of the personality:

> The Nervous Part who laughs when things are stressful
> The Pusher Part who wants things perfect and pushes you to perfectionism
> The Clumsy Part
> The Stubborn Part Who Can't Let Things Go
> The Timid Part Who is Afraid to Speak Out
> The Bossy Part who Tells Others What to Do
> The Jealous of My Brother or Sister Part
> Taking Too Much Care of Others Part
> The I-Want-It-All-for-Myself Part.

The empty bag that held the parts might become the Feeling Empty Inside Part. Choose other scruffy-looking stuffed animals to represent other parts such as a hurt part for children who have been neglected or abused. Super Hero Bear can be most sympathetic about these issues. You can use him to show that you care.

Helper Words for Children
I can find many different parts of myself. Some are funny; some are sad and feel lost.
I look for my parts that have been hiding away inside.
I can share my unhappy feelings to let them go. I share my happy feelings to feel good.
I'm feeling bad right now. I can speak, draw or write out the bad feelings to let them go.

EFT Tapping Phrases
Even though I don't like some of my parts, I'm still pretty good overall.
Even though some of my parts are hard to take, I forgive them and try to understand them.
Even though I dislike my _____ part, I am gentle with it and try to be more accepting.
Even though other people do not like my _ part, I work with it and allow it to change.
Even though I dislike my _____ part, I know it is still a part of who I am.

Tips for parents and teachers: Don't underestimate the intelligence of the children. They know about injustice even though they do not talk about the events in your group. Children can be very astute in naming the parts of themselves that carry negative self-concept messages. Children as young as three years old can identify with The Part that was Hurt by Others or The Part that Feels Bad Because Someone Touched Their Privates. One ten year old girl identified a sad little lizard as "The part that knows it was not wanted," thus revealing a hidden fear in her life and an issue to discuss with the parents. In the group setting, these painful experiences can be accepted and affirmed by an empathetic adult while teaching children new skills to cope with rejection or pain. Using these parts of the personality animals helps children move from a belief about themselves as being bad or unworthy to seeing that they have negative emotions and behaviors for which they are responsible.

Feeling Good About Learning About All of My Parts

Objective: To review all the parts.

Materials: All the stuffed animals.

Activity: I Am Many Parts:

Review all the parts with the children having them describe who each part represents and give an example of that part. Hand the appropriate stuffed animal to the child who is speaking about feelings. If the child relates that her feelings shifted while she discussed her issue, offer her other stuffed animals that represent those feelings. This first poem is for younger children; the second for older children.

Parts, parts, one, two, three,
All my parts are here with me.
Parts, parts, four, five, six,
All my parts give me kicks.
Parts, parts, seven, eight, nine,
All my parts and they are all mine!

"There's one of us that's humble;
One that's proud,
There's one that's broken hearted for his sins,
And one who, unrepentant, sits and grins.
There's one who loves his neighbor as himself,
And one who cares for naught but fame and self,
From much corroding care would I be free,
If once I could determine which is me."
Edward Sanford Martin

Questions to Generate Discussion on Parts
Which parts do you like best? Why?
Which part are you most upset with? Why? This is the part to tap on the most!
Which part do you not want to know about? Why?
Do you handle your anger in a different way now that you know about your mads?
Have you helped anyone else understand about his or her own Mad Part or Sad Part?
What was the hardest time that you shared your feelings with someone?

Questions to Generate Discussion on Helper Words
What are the best words of advice Super Hero Bear ever gave you?
What favorite Helper Words have you taught someone else?
What Helper Words do you use when you don't want to do something?
What do you say to yourself when you have done good work?
What Helper Words do you use if you start to get mad at yourself and beat yourself up?
How will you remember to keep the positive Helper Words in your brain for the rest of your life?
What Helper Words will you teach your children when you are a parent?
Trick Question: What is the best part about learning about parts?

Tips for parents and teachers: Your choosing to talk about your own parts during the day will model these concepts for the children. For example, saying "The Hurry Up Part in me wants you to quickly finish your task right now" or "The Part That Get Upset When I Hear Loud Voices is going to come out any moment now!" Children learn to accept more aspects of themselves when you are playful as you talk about your own parts and emphasize being responsible for them.

Dr. Lynne Namka is a happy psychologist and has been called "The Lady Who Knows About Mads." She is the author of the award winning web site on anger management at wwwAngriesOut.com. Her unique mission in the world is to help children and adults learn how to deal with their anger and express negative feelings in safe, constructive ways. Her book, *The Mad Family Gets Their Mads Out: Fifty Things Your Family can Say and Do to Express Anger Constructively*, which teaches the "I Formula" plus charts and activities to help children with their angry feelings, is number 23 out of the hundred best sellers on the list for domestic violence.

Mail Order Form

Name: _____ Title: _____

☐ **Purchase Order Attached** **Purchase Order Number:** _____

Billing/Ordering Address
Company: _____

Address: _____

City: _____ State/Province: _____

ZIP/Country Code: _____ Country: _____

Shipping Address

☐ **Same as Ordering Address** **Attention:** _____

Company: _____

Address: _____

City: _____ State/Province: _____

ZIP/Country Code: _____ Country: _____

Quantity	Item Description	Unit Price	Extended Price
	The Mad Family Gets Their Mads Out	$9.95	
	How To Let Go of Your Mad Baggage	$9.95	
	Avoiding Relapse: Catching Your Inner Con	$9.95	
	The Doormat Syndrome	$12.95	
	A Gathering of Grandmothers: Words of Wisdom	$15.95	
	Goodbye Ouchies & Grouchies, Hello Happy Feelings	$9.95	
	Teaching Emotional Intelligence to Children – Fifty Fun Activities for Families, Teachers and Therapists	$9.95	
	Combination – Goodbye Ouchies & Grouchies & Teaching Emotional Intelligence to Children	$17.95	

Subtotal	
Arizona Tax [Add 7%] or	
Illinois Tax [Add 6.25%]	
Shipping/Handling	
Total Payment Enclosed	

Shipping & Handling Charges
1-2 Books	$3.25
3-4 Books	$3.75
5-7 Books	$4.25
8-15 Books	$4.75

At the present time we do not accept phone, FAX or credit card orders.

For a detailed description of these items, plus curriculums on anger management skills, visit our Web Site:
www.AngriesOut.com

Schools, groups and bookstores may attach a Purchase Order and we will bill upon shipment.

Volume discounts are available to schools, nonprofit groups, bookstores and distributors.

Talk, Trust & Feel Therapeutics   5389 Golder Ranch Road   Tucson, AZ 85739 USA